# FEAST or FAMINE

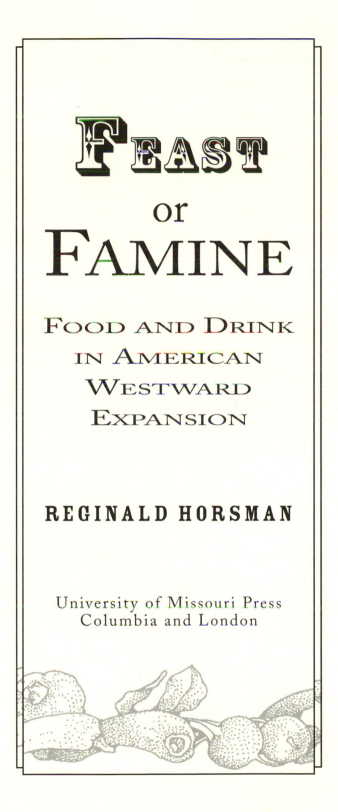

# Feast
or
# Famine

## Food and Drink in American Westward Expansion

### Reginald Horsman

University of Missouri Press
Columbia and London

Library of Congress Cataloging-in-Publication Data
Horsman, Reginald.
    Feast or famine : food and drink in American westward expansion /
Reginald Horsman.
        p. cm.
    Summary: "Drawing on the journals and correspondence of
pioneers, Horsman examines more than a hundred years of history,
recording components of the diets of various groups, including
travelers, settlers, fur traders, soldiers, and miners. He discusses food-
preparation techniques, including the development of canning, and
foods common in different regions"—Provided by publisher.
    Includes index.
    ISBN 978-0-8262-1789-9 (alk. paper)
    1. Cookery, American—Western style—History.    2. Food
habits—West (U.S.)—History—19th century.    3. Drinking
customs—West (U.S.)—History—19th century.    4. Frontier and
pioneer life—West (U.S.)    5. Overland journeys to the Pacific.
6. West (U.S.)—Discovery and exploration.    7. United
States—Territorial expansion.    I. Title.
    TX715.2.W47H67 2008
    641.5978—dc22                                        2008015259

♾™ This paper meets the requirements of the
American National Standard for Permanence of Paper
for Printed Library Materials, Z39.48, 1984.

Designer: FoleyDesign
Typesetter: The Composing Room of Michigan, Inc.
Printer and binder: Thomson-Shore, Inc.
Typeface: Adobe Caslon

The University of Missouri Press offers its grateful acknowledg-
ment to Paul Newman for his generous contribution in support of
this book and to an anonymous donor whose generous grant sup-
ports the publication of outstanding scholarship.

See p. 355 for acknowledgments and photo credits.

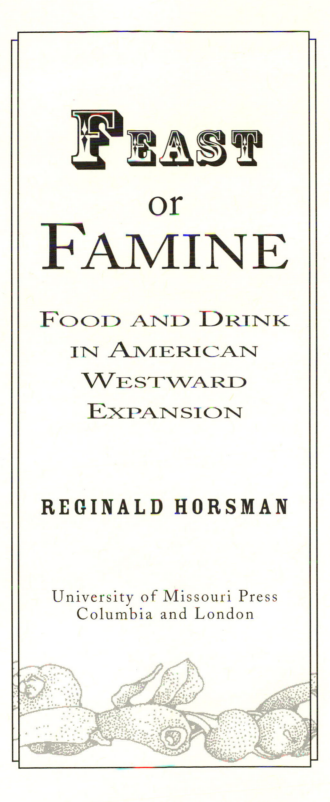

# FEAST
## or
# FAMINE

## FOOD AND DRINK
## IN AMERICAN
## WESTWARD
## EXPANSION

## REGINALD HORSMAN

University of Missouri Press
Columbia and London

Library of Congress Cataloging-in-Publication Data
Horsman, Reginald.

Feast or famine : food and drink in American westward expansion /
Reginald Horsman.

p. cm.

Summary: "Drawing on the journals and correspondence of
pioneers, Horsman examines more than a hundred years of history,
recording components of the diets of various groups, including
travelers, settlers, fur traders, soldiers, and miners. He discusses food-
preparation techniques, including the development of canning, and
foods common in different regions"—Provided by publisher.

Includes index.

ISBN 978-0-8262-1789-9 (alk. paper)

1. Cookery, American—Western style—History.   2. Food
habits—West (U.S.)—History—19th century.   3. Drinking
customs—West (U.S.)—History—19th century.   4. Frontier and
pioneer life—West (U.S.)   5. Overland journeys to the Pacific.
6. West (U.S.)—Discovery and exploration.   7. United
States—Territorial expansion.   I. Title.

TX715.2.W47H67 2008

641.5978—dc22                                           2008015259

♾™ This paper meets the requirements of the
American National Standard for Permanence of Paper
for Printed Library Materials, Z39.48, 1984.

Designer: FoleyDesign
Typesetter: The Composing Room of Michigan, Inc.
Printer and binder: Thomson-Shore, Inc.
Typeface: Adobe Caslon

The University of Missouri Press offers its grateful acknowledg-
ment to Paul Newman for his generous contribution in support of
this book and to an anonymous donor whose generous grant sup-
ports the publication of outstanding scholarship.

See p. 355 for acknowledgments and photo credits.

FOR
LENORE

# Contents

# Part 6  The Travelers

# Part 7  Conquering the Plains

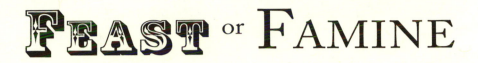

# FEAST or FAMINE

# Introduction

In our own country, the beneficial effects of a generous diet, in developing and sustaining the energies of a whole people, are clearly evident. The severe and unremitting labors of every kind, which were requisite to subdue and obtain dominion of a wilderness world could not have been done by a half-starved, suffering people.

Sarah Hale, *The Good Housekeeper,* 1841

W hile some starved, and many went hungry, most of the pioneers who settled the American continent were able to obtain a rough abundance of food. In many regions, a few basic foods—game, salt pork, corn—were essential for survival in the earliest years, but this soon changed. Remarkable agricultural expansion, and the creation of a continentwide communication system, made possible a land of plenty. The emergence of local variety was enhanced by the development of food preservation, particularly canning, and it became possible to move far beyond simple frontier foods.

In the 1870s, in the Nevada mining town of Virginia City, a woman wrote of tables laden "with food of every kind from every kingdom of the globe" and of a market that offered "everything that grows which is fit to eat and a thousand and one things which are not fit to eat." She complained of "gormandizers" bringing in special food for "their perverted tastes."[1]

Even without the wealth generated in Virginia City, it was often possible to be surprised by what was available. In 1846, when recently married Mrs. Magoffin arrived in Santa Fe with her merchant husband, her brother-in-law greeted them with champagne and oysters. Oysters were one of the early foods to be canned, and they were often stocked by western merchants in the second half of the nineteenth century. In the 1870s,

---

1. Mary M. Mathews, *Ten Years in Nevada: or Life on the Pacific Coast* (1889; repr., Lincoln: University of Nebraska Press, 1985), 171.

at Fort Lyon in Colorado, the post trader brought them in for officers' wives to buy on special occasions. More basic items were also available in substitute form. At Fort Abraham Lincoln on the Missouri River, Gen. George Custer and his wife, who lacked fresh eggs, were able to use "crystallized eggs" from airtight cans.[2]

In little over one hundred years from the end of the American Revolution, settlers spread from the Alleghenies to the Pacific. In 1783 Pittsburgh was a frontier outpost; by 1850 California was a state, and by 1900 most areas suitable for farming had been settled. Most of the settlers were farmers, but there were also explorers, trappers, soldiers, miners, and a host of other individuals. The contrasts were great—dense forests, vast plains, isolated farmsteads, frenetic mining towns, farms that had too much water, and farms that had too little. The food that was eaten varied greatly in nature, quantity, and quality, but, unlike conditions in many areas of Europe, hunger was the exception not the rule.

Americans ate well because of abundant natural resources. Vast areas of fertile land were taken from the Indians, but, even before the first crops were planted, America's riches were visible in the country's abundant wildlife. Game provided an essential element in the early diet of many settlers. In western Europe, large game was scarce and reserved for an elite. Rigid game laws provided severe punishments for those who trespassed on the lands owned by a select few. In America, as explorers and settlers advanced westward, they encountered what appeared to be an inexhaustible wildlife that was available for the taking. At times, settlers waiting for their first crops tired of endless meat and longed for bread.

In the course of crossing the continent, Americans ate a remarkable variety of game. Buffalo, venison, elk, antelope, and wild turkeys were eaten in great quantities; bear meat was common on many frontiers, and there was small game of all types, including beavers, squirrels, rabbits, opossums, and prairie chickens. Birds often darkened the skies. Wild turkeys were particularly favored, but settlers ate wild geese, ducks, and nearly everything else that flew. The rivers abounded in fish, and some pioneers ate any that they could catch, particularly catfish, pike, buffalo fish, perch, pickerel, trout, and salmon. On most frontiers, however, fish was eaten far less often than game.

2. Susan Shelby Magoffin, *Down the Santa Fe Trail, and into New Mexico: The Diary of Susan Shelby Magoffin, 1846–1847*, ed. Stella Drum (New Haven: Yale University Press, 1926), 109; Lydia Spencer Lane, *I Married a Soldier*, intro. Darlis A. Miller (1893; repr., Albuquerque: University of New Mexico Press, 1987), 28; Elizabeth B. Custer, *"Boots and Saddles," or Life in the Dakotas with General Custer*, intro. Jane Stewart (1885; repr., Norman: University of Oklahoma Press, 1966), 141.

At one time or another, meat of all types was tried and even enjoyed. The men of the Lewis and Clark Expedition dined happily on dog meat, and even Jefferson's friend and neighbor Meriwether Lewis came to like it. When George Ruxton was in the Rockies in the 1840s, he was told by the mountain men he spent time with that cougar was their favorite meat. Dog meat was a close second. It was more usual to hear trappers praising beaver tail or the choicest parts of the buffalo, although dog meat was popular with many trappers and some Indian tribes. Cougar, or mountain lion, was much rarer as a food.[3]

Wildlife was slaughtered with such reckless determination that, within a century of America's obtaining independence, some species had disappeared or were disappearing. By 1890, the buffalo (which was actually the American bison), often described by explorers as stretching in great herds across the plains to the horizon, existed only in small, scattered bands. At the time of settlement, passenger pigeons, the most numerous of all American birds, roosted in such numbers that whole stretches of forest were covered with them. Branches broke under their weight. Often they could be killed by simply knocking them from the trees with sticks. Soon after 1900, they had gone. When settlers first moved into the Mississippi valley, giant sturgeons, reaching weights of several hundred pounds, were easily caught in the Great Lakes and in the Ohio-Mississippi River systems.[4]

The reduction of wildlife went hand in hand with the bringing of great new areas of land into cultivation. Urged on by its settlers, the American government ejected the Indians from their villages, fields, and hunting grounds. Lands were cleared, crops were planted, and in many areas settlers soon had all the food they could eat. There was enough fertile land in America to provide food far beyond the needs of its settlers.

The ample game of the first years was replaced by domestic livestock. Throughout the eastern half of the country, even the poorest settlers could keep hogs, and they let them feed on the abundant resources of the woods. Well-off European travelers scoffed at westerners who seemed to have salt pork on the table at every meal, but ordinary Europeans regarded any meat as a luxury. Once the early years of settlement had passed, most American pioneers were able to eat ample beef as well as pork. Ordinary Americans were even able to indulge in large-scale likes and dislikes, and, except in the Southwest, mutton rarely found favor in the United States.

3. Gary E. Moulton, ed., *The Journals of the Lewis and Clark Expedition,* 13 vols. (Lincoln: University of Nebraska Press, 1983–2001), 6:162; George F. Ruxton, *Life in the Far West,* ed. Le Roy Hafen (Norman: University of Oklahoma Press, 1951), 76, 97–98.

4. See Peter Matthiessen, *Wildlife in America* (New York: Viking Press, 1959).

In the well-watered lands of the eastern half of the continent, vegetables became readily available soon after settlement, but they were harder to come by for the explorers and settlers of the trans-Mississippi West. Explorers, fur traders, and emigrants in western wagon trains often faced the danger of scurvy, and in the settlement of the Great Plains and the Southwest many difficulties in planting were encountered before irrigation became usual. Throughout the process of American settlement, pioneers compensated for shortages of vegetables by taking full advantage of what was available in the fields and woods.

Settlers gathered a variety of "greens"—among them purslane, nettles, lamb's quarters, dandelions, sorrel, and pigweed. They were often put into the pot with a piece of salt pork. In later years, many pioneers could happily recall childhood trips to gather berries and currants, which were available in abundance all the way across the continent. The varieties are too numerous to list in full, but among the most common were wild cherries, plums, grapes, serviceberries, gooseberries, strawberries, huckleberries, blackberries, raspberries, and elderberries. Nuts were also gathered in large quantities—walnuts, hazelnuts, hickory nuts, and butternuts were some of the favorites. Piñon nuts were a special favorite in the Southwest. Settlers replaced sugar with honey gathered from beehives in the woods, made extensive use of sugar maples, and sometimes grew sorghum cane to make sorghum molasses. When they had no tea, they made drinks of spicebrush, sage, sassafras, mint, or nettle.

A great deal has been written about the dangers that Indian resistance presented to American settlers; far less has been said about the extent to which Indian knowledge of American natural resources and their willingness to share this knowledge and their food with explorers and settlers contributed to the European settlement of the continent. For long stretches of their epic journey, Lewis and Clark depended for their very survival on food obtained from the Indians. The explorers and trappers learned from the Indians how to dig for camas, wapato, and white apple roots, as well as wild onions. Emigrants in the thousands of wagon trains that crossed the Great Plains and Rockies were very rarely attacked, but they regularly obtained food from the Indians. On the Oregon Trail, pioneers whose wagons had rolled with painful slowness across the plains were delighted to reach the Rockies and find that Indians brought large quantities of salmon to trade. On the trails of the arid Southwest, emigrants obtained grain and other crops from Indians who were engaged in extensive agriculture.

While the great mass of western settlers were able to eat in a manner that would have astounded poor Europeans, there were times, of course, when westerners went hungry or even starved. Explorers frequently ran out of food, and even trappers could not always find enough to eat. Game sometimes could be killed with the greatest of ease, but at other times could not be found. Settlers were often not skilled hunters. For most, the time until the first crops came in could be very difficult, and crops could and did fail. Some settlers, because of ill preparation, poor lands, or simply bad luck, suffered a great deal in settling the West. These individuals became more common in the latter part of the nineteenth century. Once the best areas had been occupied, settlers advanced onto marginal lands—areas with insufficient rainfall or those of searing heat or biting cold.

While some basic foods were eaten in most sections of the country, detailed diets were shaped by a variety of different conditions. Settlers who advanced onto the fertile, well-watered regions of Ohio or Kentucky ate very differently from those who first moved onto the arid, Spanish-influenced lands of the Southwest, and both groups had a very different diet from the trappers who roamed the high Rockies. The miners who flooded into California during the gold rush and soon spread throughout the Rockies at first had no desire to farm and had to depend on suppliers who usually had found a surer way to wealth than the miners themselves.

Cowboys herding cattle on long trails north from Texas, soldiers on isolated military posts, and the innumerable passengers on the coaches, steamboats, and trains of the West all formed their own patterns of diet. On the great overland trails, even careful preparation in carrying food supplies and success in hunting were often not enough to avoid hunger, or even starvation, if accidents or early snows slowed the long trek to the West Coast. Some in the seemingly well organized Donner party were reduced to cannibalism when they were trapped in the snows in the Sierras in the winter of 1846–1847.

In times of necessity, even the most unappetizing birds and animals were used as food. On one evening in the 1790s, after Oliver Spencer had been captured by Indians on the Ohio River, he and his hungry captors dined on a hawk, the only game they had been able to kill. It was plucked, singed, and boiled in a kettle with milkweed. The young shoots and leaves of the milkweed were used as a vegetable by pioneers as well as by Indians. Spencer found the tough, strong-flavored hawk practically inedible, and the saltless broth was a sad introduction to food with the Indians, but during his captivity in an Indian village in what is now northwestern Ohio, he ate well. At a feast celebrating the arrival of the green corn, he sat down to dried meat boiled with fish, stewed squirrels and venison, green corn on the cob, squash, succotash (corn and beans boiled together), roasted pumpkins, and cornmeal bread. All of these Indian dishes found favor with the pioneers.[5]

For water to drink or to cook, settlers depended on rivers and springs or on wells that had to be dug by hand. Only in the last stages of the settlement of the continent did well-digging equipment become available, and even then most people could not afford to hire it. Settlers in the eastern half of the Mississippi valley often made use of river water in the early years, although on the lower Mississippi a glass of water had to be left before drinking to allow the abundant silt to settle. On the Great Plains and in the Southwest finding enough water to drink or to use in cooking was often a problem. Even when wells were dug, they often went dry.

Patterns of western eating obviously had endless individual variations, particularly ethnic, and I have made no attempt at the impossible task of discussing them all, nor have I attempted to discuss the varied and complex diets of the hundreds of Indian tribes. Indian foods, ethnic foods, and the diet of slaves on the frontier south of the Ohio need their own books. My emphasis is on broad differences in eating patterns at the different stages of the advance westward, particularly on how specific individuals ate from day to day. Fortunately, many found the experience of creating a new life on new lands so remarkable that they were inspired to leave a written record of how they lived.[6]

5. Milo M. Quaife, ed., *The Indian Captivity of O. M. Spencer* (1835; repr. Chicago: R. R. Donnelley, 1917), 71–72, 106–7.

6. For Colonial America, there is a full discussion of the impact of Native American and African slave food on the diet of the various regions in James E. McWilliams, *A Revolution in Eating: How the Quest for Food Shaped America* (New York: Columbia University Press, 2005).

# *Part 1*

## Forest and Prairie

CHAPTER 1

# Food in the Forest

I cannot help here describing the amazing plenty and variety of this nights supper. We had fine roast buffalo beef, soup of buffalo beef and turkeys, fried turkeys, fried catfish, fresh caught, roast ducks, good punch, madeira, claret, grog and toddy.

Richard Butler, along the Ohio River, 1785

In the years immediately prior to the American Revolution, the first pioneers crossed the Alleghenies and began the advance across the Mississippi valley. They moved into a great forest that stretched as far as the eye could see. There were a few natural clearings, and some areas where the Indians had cleared lands for their own crops, but families headed west often trudged for days in the shade of trees. The difficulties and advantages of this forest dominated the supply of food as pioneers began to settle the Mississippi valley. There was often abundant game, and hogs grew fat foraging on the rich accumulation of nuts on the forest floor, but before crops could be planted and regular food provided, the land had to be at least partially cleared.

Both explorers and settlers were overwhelmed by the richness of the region. Deer, elk, and bears were all present in large numbers along the Ohio River, and at times the skies were darkened by great flocks of wild turkeys and passenger pigeons. Raccoons, opossums, panthers, wildcats, wolves, foxes, and innumerable squirrels added to the mix. On the eve of the Revolution a traveler who visited a settlement near the mouth of the Kentucky River wrote that a man could kill six or eight deer every day. Venison and turkey were eaten most often, but in times of necessity any game was used to stave off hunger.[1]

In these first years, there were still large herds of buffalo in the areas

1. J. Ferdinand Smyth, *A Tour in the United States of America,* 2 vols. (London, 1784), 1:337–38.

immediately west of the mountains. A hunter told early Kentucky settler and historian John Filson that he had seen over a thousand buffalo at the Kentucky Blue Licks at one time. There were so many that the first settlers "wantonly sported away their lives." As late as 1792 eight buffalo were shot near Marietta in southeast Ohio, but as settlement increased, buffalo became increasingly rare. By 1802 French traveler François Michaux reported that though buffalo had once been abundant in Kentucky, they had now practically disappeared, and those that were left had retreated to the east bank of the Mississippi. Wild turkeys had also became less common.[2]

Fish abounded in the Ohio and its tributaries. Huge pike and catfish were pulled from the Ohio in the first years of settlement, and there was a great variety of other fish—salmon, buffalo fish, sturgeon, and perch were often mentioned. Writing from Fort McIntosh on the Ohio in 1785, Col. Josiah Harmar said that the contractor was failing to supply beef, but there was an abundance of fish. "What think you," he wrote, "of pike of 25 lbs.; perch of 15 to 20 lbs.; cat-fish of 40 lbs; bass, pickerel, sturgeon etc. etc." For dessert there were wild strawberries, which "luxuriantly covered" the ground around the fort. There were so many, Harmar said, he was "almost surfeited with them."[3]

In 1785, when Indian commissioner Richard Butler was on the Ohio River just below the mouth of the Great Kanawha, he wrote that he had only had to jump from their boat to be among flocks of turkeys. Bears were growling within his hearing, and deer were bounding along in full view. His party feasted "on fine venison, bear meat, turkeys and catfish, procured by themselves at pleasure." One supper amazed him in its "plenty and variety. They had "fine roast buffalo beef, soup of buffalo beef and turkeys, fried turkeys, fried cat fish, fresh caught, roast ducks, good punch, madeira, claret, grog, and toddy." They had brought the drinks with them, but the food had all come from hunting and fishing.[4]

When settlers arrived in these eastern woodlands, they first depended on

2. John Filson, *The Discovery, Settlement, and Present State of Kentucke* (1784; repr., Ann Arbor: University Microfilms, 1966), 27–28; "Two Western Journeys of John Filson, 1785," ed. Beverley Bond Jr., *Mississippi Valley Historical Review,* 9 (1923): 324; Samuel P. Hildreth, *Pioneer History* (Cincinnati, 1848), 496–99; John Heckewelder, *Thirty Thousand Miles with John Heckewelder,* ed. Paul A. W. Wallace (Pittsburgh: University of Pittsburgh Press, 1958), 226, 228–31, 291; François A. Michaux, "Travels West of the Alleghany Mountains, 1802," in *Early Western Travels, 1748–1846,* ed. Reuben G. Thwaites, 32 vols. (Cleveland: A. H. Clark, 1904–1907), 3:234–36.

3. Harmar to Thomas Mifflin, June 25, 1785, in Consul W. Butterfield, *The Journal of Capt. Jonathan Heart* (Albany, N.Y., 1885), 74–76; Heckewelder, *Thirty Thousand Miles,* 228.

4. "Journal of General [Richard] Butler," in *The Olden Time,* ed. Neville B. Craig, 2 vols. (1848; repr., Cincinnati, 1876), 2:447–48.

the food they brought with them and on the game they could hunt. This was not always easy, for game was frightened away from the areas being settled, and many pioneers did not have the necessary skills for successful hunting. Those who came down the Ohio River on rafts, or used wagons on wilderness roads, tried to bring at least a barrel of corn flour, a barrel of salt pork, additional salt, and perhaps dried beans. The poorest came on foot and could bring only what they could carry. For most early settlers, the food supply was precarious until land could be cleared and the first crop of corn planted and raised. If all went well, pioneers had a crop of corn in the year after settling.

Clearing the land occupied endless hours. Small trees that could be felled with an axe were chopped down; the larger were girdled by cutting deep gashes completely around the trunks so that the trees slowly died. Underbrush was gathered and burned. Corn was planted amid the stumps and larger dying trees. Sometimes corn received too much shade from the dying leaves of the girdled trees, but in the well-watered, fertile soil of the Ohio valley region settlers could usually expect a good crop. Like all farmers, however, they were vulnerable to natural disasters.

Salt pork and corn were the basic foods of the Ohio valley pioneers, supplemented in the first years by large quantities of game. There was no wheat bread in the early years except when some of the more prosperous settlers bought wheat flour from boats that came from Pennsylvania to trade along the Ohio River. Wheat would not grow well in the rich soil until there had been successive crops of corn. Many settlers, especially recent emigrants from England where corn bread was unknown, very much missed wheat flour, and the lighter, whiter bread it made possible; however, corn remained dominant. At first, other crops were extremely limited. Most common were beans, which were planted so that they could climb the stems of the corn, pumpkins, melons, and cucumbers. Turnips were often planted on the corn land after the corn had been picked.

Practically all of the settlers got a few hogs as soon as they could. The hogs were allowed to forage for themselves in the woods, but those destined for slaughter were often brought in during the fall to be fattened on corn. Slaughtering usually took place in December. Some choice cuts and the liver from each hog were cooked and eaten immediately, and meat was often chopped to make sausages (using the intestines as a casing), but most of the meat was preserved. If possible, a side was cured and smoked to make bacon, and a hind leg cured and smoked for a ham, but most pieces were rubbed with salt, placed in a barrel, and immersed in a brine solution. One brine recipe called for six pounds of salt, one pound of sugar, and four ounces of saltpeter. This was boiled in four gallons of water and skimmed before meat was immersed in it. A board with a weight on it was used to keep the pieces submerged.[5]

The pork barrel became a standard feature of settler life throughout the nineteenth century. The state of preservation depended on the amount of salt that had been available and the care that had been taken in preparation. When a piece was pulled out to be cooked, it was wiped off and ideally soaked in water for hours or overnight to reduce the salt, but some people omitted the soaking. It was often simply cut into rough pieces and fried or perhaps boiled in a pot with corn or with "greens" gathered in the woods. Whether it came from the barrel, or had been cut from a side that had been cured and smoked, it was usually referred to not as pork but as "bacon." In nutritional terms, pork provided the settlers with a good range of B vitamins, particularly thiamin, niacin, and B-6.

No part of the pig was wasted. Meat taken from the head was used to make head cheese. For this, the meat was chopped, seasoned, put in a sticky broth, cooked in a mold, and allowed to set before being sliced. With what was left—particularly the ears, nose, and feet—the settlers often made souse. For this, the parts were soaked in frequently changed water until all the blood was drawn away. They were then scraped, cleaned, boiled with a little cornmeal in salted water until all the bones came out, seasoned, sewed tightly into a cloth, and soaked in a mixture of water and vinegar. This marinade was changed every two or three weeks.[6]

Hog fat, particularly that taken from around the internal organs, was rendered to make lard. When it had cooled and set in a solid white mass, it was saved for use in frying and baking. In later years, old pioneers remembered their delight as children when they were given an early version of crullers or doughnuts deep-fried in the fresh lard. One fancy early-nineteenth-century Virginia recipe for "Dough Nuts—A Yankee Cake" called for half a pound of pounded brown sugar mixed with two pounds of flour, yeast, milk, and butter. The sugar had to be pounded because in the early nineteenth century much of the sugar that was bought was raw. Before sugar-refining machinery was developed, refining doubled the cost. After the sugar was combined with the flour, the mixture was sifted, yeast and milk were added, and, when the dough had risen, half a pound of butter was kneaded in. Pieces were pulled off and dropped into the boiling fat.

5. *Mackenzie's Five Thousand Recipes* (Pittsburgh, 1831), 399; Mary Randolph, *Virginia House-Wife: or Methodical Cook* (1824; repr., Columbia, S.C.: Dover Publications, 1984), 17–19.
6. Randolph, *Virginia House-Wife,* 20–21.

Doughnuts with holes came later; frontier families had simpler versions—"sweet compounds of flour and milk & spices."[7]

In the early years of settlement, cattle were less common than hogs, and sheep were rare. Sheep fared much less well than hogs on rough, recently settled lands, and they were very vulnerable to the many wolves. Mutton was disliked by most Ohio valley settlers. In Kentucky, cattle thrived in the abundant canebrakes. When increased settlement exhausted the brakes, farmers planted timothy seed to provide small meadows for hay. Families with children tried to keep at least one cow for milk, and if there was enough milk, the mother of the family usually made butter, and sometimes cheese. As settlement increased, butter and cheese were often sold in the nearest village or town. All across America, this became a way for frontier women to earn a little pocket money, and for many it was an important addition to family income.

In 1788, young Daniel Drake moved to Kentucky with his family and several other settlers from New Jersey. Later in life, Drake, who became a famous western physician, described his early years in letters to his children. From 1788 to 1800 he lived in a log cabin some eight miles from the village of Washington. The settlers from New Jersey had bought a tract of land, and they called their new settlement Mayslick. In the late summer of 1788 the Drakes moved into a log cabin built by their father. They quickly cleared enough land to plant corn and a few vegetables, and, while waiting for their first crops, lived mostly on game, usually venison or wild turkeys.[8]

Along with most other settlers in the region, Drake's family suffered a disaster at the end of August 1789 when the first crop of corn was killed by an early frost. They had already lived for fourteen months with little but game to eat, and now they had to wait until the following year for a corn crop. Surprisingly, although they wearied of the constant venison and turkey, they did not make any regular use of the well-stocked rivers. This was typical of many Kentucky farm families. Drake commented that his family "cloyed on animal food" and came near to loathing it. Deer, he wrote, were numerous, and wild turkeys "numberless."[9]

James Finley, whose family moved to Kentucky a few years before the

7. Ibid., 160; Daniel Drake, *Pioneer Life in Kentucky, 1785–1800*, ed. Emmet F. Horine (1870; repr., New York: H. Schuman, 1948), 99; James E. Nichols, "The Grocery Trade," in *1795–1895: One Hundred Years of American Commerce*, ed. Chauncey M. Depew (New York, 1895), 587–98.

8. Drake, *Pioneer Life*, 7–15, 24–25.

9. Ibid., 25.

Drakes, wrote that game was the principal subsistence for the early settlers. "Wild meat," he wrote, "without bread or salt, was often their food
for weeks together." Although fish was never as important as meat to the
pioneers, some people took advantage of what was available. In 1784, at the
falls of the Ohio (modern Louisville), Henry Muhlenberg and his friends
varied bear meat, venison, and turkey with fish. They took turns at hunting and fishing.[10]

Even after settlers had raised their first crops, hunting still provided an
important part of their diet. Deer continued to be easiest to find, but there
were still numerous bears. Some pioneers made bacon out of the bear
meat—removing the fat, salting the meat, and hanging it up to smoke.
The fat was rendered and saved. It replaced or supplemented butter or hog
lard, was used to fry venison and turkey, and was also mixed with dried
buffalo meat ("jerky") and parched corn. Occasionally, settlers ate mountain lion, which was usually known as panther in Kentucky. Some liked it.
Of the smaller game, wild turkeys continued to be important, and raccoon,
opossum, groundhog, and squirrels were often eaten. Wolf and wildcat
(bobcat) were only used when nothing else was available.[11]

The rapid growth of Kentucky's population in the 1790s made large
game much scarcer near to the well-settled areas. Small game, attracted by
the new crops, continued to be readily available, and squirrels became a
menace to the corn crop throughout the Ohio valley region. Squirrel hunting, like corn-husking or cabin-raising, became a communal activity in
which groups of men competed for the biggest kill. It helped save the crops
and provided a popular food. Later in the nineteenth century, one version,
cooked with a variety of vegetables and other meats, became well known
as Brunswick stew.[12]

In the early years, the settlers often lacked salt to use with their game.
Salt brought in from the East was expensive, and it was difficult to make
enough at local salt licks. Salt licks were located where natural salt springs
or deposits of rock salt attracted animals. The major Kentucky source was
at the Blue Licks, where eight hundred gallons of water had to be boiled
down to obtain one bushel of salt. Pioneers who lacked salt very much
missed its flavor, but a more serious problem was that a regular supply was

10. James B. Finley, *Autobiography of Rev. James B. Finley, or, Pioneer Life in the West,* ed. W. P.
Strickland (Cincinnati, 1853), 69, 71, 74, 79–84, 87–88, 93–96, 148–49; Henry A. Muhlenberg's
journal, in Henry A. Muhlenberg, *The Life of Major-General Peter Muhlenberg of the Revolutionary
Army* (Philadelphia, 1849), 438.
11. Finley, *Autobiography,* 73–96.
12. Drake, *Pioneer Life,* 130–31.

needed to preserve food—not only game or fish, but also the essential pork. As settlement along the Ohio increased, much salt was brought in from a large salt lick located where the Great Kanawha flows into the Ohio River (in modern West Virginia). This lick began to be used commercially in the late 1790s, and within twenty years over fifty salt producers were located there.[13]

Salt was essential in December at hog killing time, when pork was preserved for the coming year. That was also the time for special treats. Daniel Drake's happiest memories of the hog killing season were sausages, doughnuts and "wonders" fried in the fresh lard, and mince pies. As a boy, he cut up the fat and helped to chop meat for sausages. These were hung on poles for "moderate smoke drying" before frying. "In those days of simple fare," wrote Drake, "the annual return of the sausage season was hailed by the whole family." "Wonders" were what later became known as crullers. The pies were a simple version of old-fashioned mince pies, and meat was an important ingredient—in this case, finely chopped pork. Other ingredients had to be used sparingly. In the first years, apples were "too 'dear' and scarce" to be used in any quantity.[14]

Meat in early-nineteenth-century mince pies was more often beef or neat's foot (the foot of an ox). In her 1796 cookbook, Amelia Simmons had recipes both for "*Minced Pies. A Foot Pie*," and for "*Minced Pie of Beef*." For the first, the feet had to be scalded, cleaned, put in regularly changed water for a week, boiled, deboned, and, when cold, chopped fine. Four pounds of the minced meat was mixed with a pound of beef suet, four pounds of chopped apples, a little salt, a quart of wine, two pounds of stoned raisins, an ounce of cinnamon, and an ounce of mace, and sweetening to one's taste. The second recipe was similar, with four pounds of finely chopped boiled beef replacing the neats' feet, six instead of four pounds of chopped raw apples, and a suggestion that sweet cider could be used in place of the wine. In both cases the mixture was placed in a pastry of flour, butter (three-quarters the weight of the flour), and eggs. Simmons was planning a considerable quantity, as her recipe called for twelve eggs to a peck of the flour and butter. A peck amounted to about eight quarts dry or two gallons wet measure.[15]

13. Drake, *Pioneer Life*, 31, 61; Hildreth, *Pioneer History*, 405; Julia P. Butler, *Life and Times of Ephraim Cutler* (1890; repr., New York: Arno Press, 1971); 31; Muhlenberg, *Life*, 447; Mark Kurlansky, *Salt: A World History* (New York: Walker and Company, 2002), 249–55.

14. Drake, *Pioneer Life*, 98–99.

15. Amelia Simmons, *The First American Cookbook: A Facsimile of "American Cookery," 1796*, intro. Mary Tolford Wilson (1958; repr., New York: Dover Publications, 1984), 23–24, 29.

Drake's family, like many of the other settlers, made butter and cheese. Drake remembered the long, hard churning to make butter and also recalled, with more pleasure, making cheese; helping his mother as "right hand man" by preparing the rennet and helping to squeeze the whey from the curds. Rennet, taken from a calf's stomach, was used to curdle the milk.[16]

Above all else, corn is central to Daniel Drake's account of food in his childhood. Corn is a good source of the B vitamins, vitamin C, and potassium, and yellow corn also has some vitamin A. Corn also provides a reasonable amount of plant protein, although it lacks some of the essential amino acids. Corn was a basic settler food, but long before the Europeans came to America, the Indians had developed ways of preparing and eating corn that much increased its nutritional value. One of the most important of the Indian dishes was succotash, and this was eagerly taken up by the settlers. Fresh corn and beans were cooked separately and then mixed, sometimes with the addition of a little butter or salt pork. The amino acids in beans, which are rich in niacin and folic acid, complement those in corn.[17]

Another problem with the nutritional value of corn is that its rich niacin content is bound in compounds that make it largely unavailable to humans, but when corn is prepared as hominy, the niacin is released. Hominy, like succotash, was used by the Indians before the Europeans came to America. Pioneers prepared hominy by first drying the corn and removing the hulls. Sometimes the hulling was done by grinding the kernels in a mortar and either winnowing or using boiling water to remove the hulls, but more often the corn was boiled with wood ashes. Lye released by the boiling softened the hulls so that they could be removed easily.

Settlers made various mushes and puddings with hominy by boiling it with water or milk, and in the South the dried kernels were often ground, boiled, and served as "grits." James Finley, who said hominy was a good substitute for bread, remembered Kentucky pioneers mixing their hominy with raccoon or opossum oil. Pioneer children, and often others in the family, ate corn mush and milk for breakfast. For this, corn was pounded,

---

16. Drake, *Pioneer Life*, 96, 98.

17. There is an extensive discussion of corn in history in Betty Fussell, *The Story of Corn* (New York: North Point Press, 1992). Nutritional aspects of corn, and other foods, are well treated in brief in Carol Ann Rinzler, *The Complete Book of Food* (New York: World Almanac, 1987). See also *The Oxford Encyclopedia of Food and Drink in America*, 2 vols. (New York: Oxford University Press, 2004), 1: 341–44.

boiled, and mixed with milk. It was also often cooked with a piece of salt pork. For boiling, foods were placed in a pot and hung over an open fire at the end of the cabin.[18]

As the corn began to grow, Drake and the other children had the job of keeping off the marauding squirrels and crows. When the crops ripened, settlers, like the Indians, delighted in the milky roasting ears. Drake writes of "the daily feast" of green corn, which began as soon as the grains were half grown. It continued until no more "milk" would flow out when kernels were pierced with a thumbnail. Drake's first task in the morning was to gather and husk enough corn for breakfast, which the family would eat with milk fresh from their cow.[19]

Although corn was eaten in a variety of ways, its lack of gluten made it unsuitable for leavened bread. The basic bread was in the form of "Johnnycakes," which were given different names—ash cakes, hoecakes, Indian pone, or simply pone—at different times and in different places. Amelia Simmons, in her *American Cookery*, gave two recipes for *"Johny Cake, or Hoe Cake."* One recipe called for putting one pint of scalded milk in with three pints of cornmeal and half a pint of flour. In the other, the milk, or boiling water, was added to two-thirds of the cornmeal, with salt, molasses, and shortening, and kneaded with cold water until it was "pretty stiff." In both cases, the resulting dough was placed on a board and baked before the fire. When one side was baked, the bread was turned over. Johnnycakes were eaten with most meals.[20]

Kentucky soil was not particularly hospitable to wheat, and Drake's parents, like many other settlers, very much missed wheat bread. After a few years, they planted enough wheat to meet their own needs.[21]

Grinding corn was a problem in the early years. The simplest method used mortar and pestle. Corn was placed in a hollow that had been burnt into a flat section of a tree trunk, and it was then pounded with an iron wedge in a wooden handle. Boiling water was added and the corn hulls removed. Some had a hand-mill, in which the upper of two millstones was turned by means of a rod running upward through a hole in the stone. The first public water mills were expensive, and drought meant that the mills stopped turning. To avoid this, mills driven by horsepower were used, and settlers along the Ohio River also made use of floating mills that were

18. Fussell, *Story of Corn*, 175, 195–200; *Autobiography of Finley*, 69.
19. Drake, *Pioneer Life*, 50–53.
20. Simmons, *First American Cookbook*, 34.
21. Ibid., 63–64.

anchored in the river itself and driven by the power of the current. In the early years these floating mills had the additional advantage of being more easily protected from Indian attack.[22]

The early Tennesseans had much the same diet as their neighbors to the north. As late as 1799, agriculture in the Cumberland settlements of west Tennessee, a region that soon became a major cotton producer, was said to consist mainly of raising corn. Not much wheat was grown, and there was little variety in vegetables. Venison, bear, squirrel, and pork were the main meats. There were few cattle. In 1797, a traveler near Nashville was given a large piece of boiled bacon, a dish of beans, and corn bread for an evening meal. On another day his supper consisted of "nothing but some Indian bread and butter, and some milk, which is a standing dish in all these new countries." For breakfast, he had fried rashers of bacon, corn bread, and coffee.[23]

In east Tennessee there were more cattle, wheat, rye, and oats than in the Cumberland region, but corn was still the basic crop, and coming from west Tennessee the traveler found his meals were very much the same. When he stopped for the night, the family was sitting down to a soup "made by boiling Indian corn and bacon together, or in some such way."[24]

Although game, pork, and corn were basic foods throughout the region, Drake's Kentucky reminiscences reveal the efforts made by these early Mississippi valley pioneers to acquire variety. From an early date the Drakes grew turnips, potatoes, and cucumbers. Drake remembered sitting by the fire on winter evenings scraping and eating turnips. As a substitute for candlelight, the fire was brightened with pieces of hickory bark. The family also had watermelons and muskmelons, and, like most of their neighbors, they grew pumpkins. Before there was any cultivated fruit, pumpkins and wild berries were the main standby for pies. Pumpkins were dried and stored for winter use, and pumpkin juice was boiled down to make a type of molasses.[25]

The surrounding fields and forests also added variety to the Drakes' table. After a long winter of corn, salt pork, and game, with perhaps a few

22. Ibid., 114–15; Finley, *Autobiography,* 69, 73; Isaac J. Finley and Rufus Putnam, *Record and Reminiscences of the Early Settlers and Settlement of Ross County, Ohio* (Cincinnati, 1871), 6; Hildreth, *Pioneer History,* 375–77; *The Journal of Andrew Ellicot* (Philadelphia, 1803), 11–12; Christian Schultz Jr., *Travels on an Inland Voyage . . . in the years 1807 and 1808,* 2 vols. (New York, 1810), 1: 189; Drake, *Pioneer Life,* 57–60.

23. Francis Baily, *Journal of a Tour in the Unsettled Parts of North America in 1796 and 1797,* ed. Jack D. L. Holmes (1856; repr., Carbondale: Southern Illinois University, 1969), 409–10, 417–18, 423.

24. Michaux, "Travels," in *Early Western Travels,* 3:280–82; Baily, *Journal,* 438; Henry Ker, *Travels through the Western Interior of the United States* (Elizabethtown, N. J., 1816), 21–22.

25. Drake, *Pioneer Life,* 24, 46–48.

turnips and potatoes, settlers looked forward to spring and the availability of "greens." Nettles and purslane were popular choices. The young shoots and leaves of the nettles were boiled. This neutralized the acid that made them sting. They were cooked in a pot with a piece of salt pork to provide a nutritious meal. Purslane was eaten both cooked and raw, and, if no cucumbers were available, purslane stems could be pickled. Settlers did not know it, but the fleshy leaves of purslane gave them iron, potassium, and magnesium, as well as the fatty acid omega-3. At times, when food had run short, nettles, purslane, and other greens were used to stave off hunger rather than provide variety.

Many settlers believed that the phases of the moon affected both their crops and their animals. Crops like radishes, which tapered downward, were planted when the moon was waning; some other crops were planted when it was waxing. It was argued that if hogs were slaughtered in the dark, or when the moon was waning, the pork would shrink and waste away in the barrel. Astrology was also used, and almanacs containing information on the signs of the zodiac found a place in many frontier cabins. Drake said almanacs were consulted before a baby was weaned. Thirty years later an English settler in Illinois was struck by the way that Americans planted according to the phases of the moon. Many of them he wrote "are very superstitious."

They may have been superstitious, but they were keeping up English practices that were apparently unknown to this English settler. In Elizabethan England, one of the most popular agricultural guidebooks advised sowing when the moon was waxing and gathering when the moon was waning.[26]

The first orchards in the Ohio valley were made up of peach trees, for these would bear within three years. Apart from the fruit eaten directly from the trees, the settlers made a great quantity of peach brandy. Apple, pear, and cherry trees were slower to arrive, but farmers often planted them once they were well settled. Settlers also made much use of fruits available to them in the woods. Women and children gathered huckleberries, which are very much like blueberries but with a tougher skin and not quite as sweet. They also collected pawpaws, which are bananalike with a pale yellow flesh filled with seeds. Haws, small red berries, were too tart for immediate eating and, like crab apples, were usually used to make jam or jelly. Children ate honey locust pods, as they contained a sweet pulp. Wild grapes and nuts were often stored for winter use.

26. Ibid., 204–5; John Woods, *Two Years Residence on the English Prairie of Illinois,* ed. Paul M. Angle (1822; repr., Chicago: Lakeside Press, 1968), 156; Gamino Salgado, *The Elizabethan Underworld* (1977; repr., Stroud, England: Sutton Publishing, 1992), 93–94.

In Drake's area, black walnuts were the most abundant nuts, but his family also collected hickory nuts and butternuts. The hulls had to be removed and the shells broken (often a considerable problem with the very hard-shelled hickory), but cracking and eating nuts was a pastime on winter evenings. Nuts were gathered in the early fall, one hoped before the squirrels could get at them, and sometimes they were pickled.

Sugar was not readily available, but sugar maples and beehives were common throughout the eastern half of the Mississippi valley. Drake's family had only a few sugar maples on their property, but his father rented a sugar camp about two miles away. In the late winter Daniel worked with his father to lay in a good supply of syrup for the coming year. While at the camp they made a "spicewood tea" with maple syrup and milk, which they brought with them. Tapping sugar maples in late winter was a regular settler activity. Settlers also traveled long distances to locate beehives for honey.[27]

Tea and coffee, even if available, were expensive items for early settlers, and they often used substitutes. Parched corn was one possibility. In 1784, at the falls of the Ohio, Henry Muhlenberg rose at daybreak and drank parched corn mixed with water as a substitute for coffee. Among the substitutes for normal tea were spicebush, sage, sassafras, and nettles. Spicebush leaves were used for tea-making in the spring, and the twigs and bark could be used to make tea during the rest of the year. Many settlers developed a taste for sassafras tea. This could be made either from the dried leaves or the boiled roots. Sage, when it was available, made a tea that was used for colds. It was even said that the sweet seeds and pulp in the pods of the honey locust made excellent "beer."[28]

Whiskey—not beer—was the most common drink in the early years of Ohio valley settlement. Travelers often commented on the hard liquor that accompanied the constant diet of salt pork and corn. Whiskey and peach brandy were made as soon as corn and peaches were available. In both cases the distilled product was much easier to transport and sell than the bulk crop, and a surplus could be kept on hand for personal use or later sale. It could also be used for trade. On one occasion, Daniel Drake's father sold a horse, and he took one hundred gallons of whiskey in partial payment. The Drakes sold whiskey to their neighbors, who sent their young sons with bottles or jugs. In most frontier families, the whiskey bottle was always

27. Drake, *Pioneer Life*, 86–87, 127–29; Filson, *Kentucke*, 23.

28. Muhlenberg, *Life of Muhlenberg*, 447; Drake, *Pioneer Life*, 87; Peter Cartwright, *The Backwood's Preacher: An Autobiography of Peter Cartwright*, ed. W. P. Strickland (London, 1858), 6–7; Filson, *Kentucke*, 23.

kept refilled for those who might call. The only abstainers were a few families of Methodists.[29]

Alcohol was accepted as part of the daily routine of these early frontiersmen. It was said that a "a house could not be raised, a field of wheat cut down, nor could there be a log rolling, a husking, a quilting, a wedding, or a funeral without the aid of alcohol." In 1806, an unfriendly British visitor commented that Kentuckians ate salt meat three times a day and drank ardent spirits from morning to night. He praised very little, but in one log cabin where he visited he enjoyed a drink made of whiskey, peach juice, sugar, and water, and lavished praise on a tureen of squirrel broth. His host confined himself to eating salt pork and drinking whiskey.[30]

While liquor was readily available, it was not always a simple matter to supply water for drinking and cooking, even on the well-watered Ohio valley frontier. The Drakes had a small spring near their cabin and also collected water in a trough under the cabin's eaves, but in periods of drought, the spring did not supply enough water and at times went dry. Young Drake then brought water from a permanent spring half a mile away. The family also made use of a pond about a mile away both for watering stock and for washing clothes.[31]

Many Kentucky inhabitants, except those in the vicinity of the big rivers, suffered in summer from a lack of water. Those close to the Ohio took most of their water from that river. In 1811, a visitor to Washington, Kentucky, noticed that the supply there was so inadequate that sometimes water had to be brought four miles from the Ohio River in carts. In Ohio, Cincinnati residents also used the river for most of their water. At times, Drake's father thought of moving north of the Ohio. He gave as his reasons: slavery in Kentucky, the uncertainty of land titles, and the want of good water.[32]

While Daniel Drake, like so many other pioneers, remembered a difficult early life, he had pleasant memories of family meals. There were mornings with a fire burning, a johnnycake set near it to bake on a clean board,

29. Drake, *Pioneer Life*, 84–85.

30. Finley, *Autobiography*, 248; Cartwright, *Autobiography*, 11; Michaux, "Travels," in *Early Western Travels*, 3:144; Thomas Ashe, *Travels in America Performed in 1806*, 2 vols. (London, 1808), 2:280–81.

31. Drake, *Pioneer Life*, 80–81, 96.

32. Ibid., 209; Michaux, "Travels," in *Early Western Travels*, 3:223–24; John Melish, *Travels in the United States of America in the Years 1806 and 1807, and 1809, 1810, and 1811*, 2 vols. (Philadelphia, 1812), 2:200; Schultz, *Travels*, 1:140–41; Daniel Drake, *Natural and Statistical View, or Picture of Miami and the Miami Country* (Cincinnati, 1815), 139.

and a tea kettle swinging from a pole. Daniel turned the meat frying in a pan, watched the johnnycake, or set the table. His sister dressed the smaller children, and when all was ready, Daniel blew in a conch shell to call their father, who was already working in the cornfield. The family gathered round their table for a blessing, and there was a "dull clatter of pewter spoons in pewter basins" as they finally sat down to breakfast. The pewter and their tin cups were fixed by a traveling tinker, who stayed the night before he soldered the cracks and turned "old pewter basins into new."[33]

In the 1780s and 1790s, while individual Kentuckians began to make new lives south of the Ohio, a more organized settlement took place north of the river in what became the southeastern corner of the state of Ohio. In April 1788 the Ohio Company brought a pioneer party of fewer than fifty New Englanders to found the settlement of Marietta on the Ohio River at the mouth of the Muskingum. The party that landed there brought supplies of flour, beans, salt, and a few other supplies to sustain them in their first months. At first, prospects were good. The land they had chosen was fertile, and by June, through backbreaking labor, they had managed to clear over 130 acres. They planted crops typical of early settlement throughout the region: corn, potatoes, turnips, pumpkins, squashes, cabbages, melons, beans, and cucumbers. At first, there was also abundant game. One settler commented in July that deer were more numerous in the area than horned cattle were in New England.

On July 4, 1788, the whole settlement sat down in "a long bower'y" to venison, bear meat, buffalo meat, pork, wild turkey and other fowl, a variety of fish, vegetables, punch, and wine. The New Englanders made more use of the abundant fish than the Kentuckians, but even here fish did not become a basic part of the diet for most settlers. The pork for the celebration had been obtained from small settlements on the opposite bank of the Ohio in what much later was to become West Virginia. The frontiersmen there had far more experience than the New Englanders, and they provided hunters as well as some supplies.[34]

Unlike Drake's family in Kentucky, the New Englanders had reasonable luck with their first corn and vegetable crops, although the corn crop was reduced by the shade of the leaves that clung to the girdled trees. As the

33. Drake, *Pioneer Life*, 107–8, 224–25.
34. Hildreth, *Pioneer History*, 204–26; John May, *The Western Journals of John May* (Cincinnati: Historical and Philosophical Society of Ohio, 1961), 46–63. Much of this material in this section on the Marietta region was first used, in somewhat different form, in Reginald Horsman, "Hunger in a Land of Plenty: Marietta's Lean Years," *Timeline* 19 (2002): 20–31.

newcomers settled in for the winter of 1788–1789, most of the supplies they had brought with them had run out. They depended on the new crops they had raised and on game, but game had suddenly become scarce in the immediate vicinity of Marietta.

In the summer of 1788, hundreds of Indians had gathered at Fort Muskingum, across the Muskingum River from Marietta, to sign treaties with the American government. They had hoped to persuade the government to cancel land cessions north of the Ohio that had been forced from them a few years earlier. Instead, the federal negotiators angered the Indians by insisting on a confirmation of the earlier cessions. When the Indians first arrived, they killed large quantities of game for their own use, and, after the disappointing treaties were signed, they set about slaughtering all the game they could find, leaving it to rot in the woods. A settler later commented that the Indians "meant to destroy & Starve out every white face North of the Ohio." Some venison and bear meat were obtained that winter, but by March food was very scarce. The settlers lived on what they had left of their corn, supplemented by what they could gather in the woods.[35]

After surviving the first winter, the settlers were hopeful that their main problems in providing food were over. In reality, they were just beginning. In the spring and summer of 1789 new settlers continued to arrive, and there was expansion into areas close to Marietta—to Belpre on the Ohio, and some twenty miles up the Muskingum to Waterford. More land was cleared and planted, but the corn crop in Marietta and Belpre was hurt by an early frost. The corn was gathered and stored, but most of it became moldy. Some of it was ground and made into bread, but those who ate it usually vomited.[36]

By midwinter, food shortages were so severe that the settlers again tried to use some of the moldy corn. Charles Devoll, whose family lived at Belpre, remembered his father returning from Marietta with a little of the corn after the family had been without bread for two days. They mixed it with fresh juice from the maple trees and made it into "sap porridge," a dish regarded as a treat when it was made with sound corn. But this was moldy corn, and the children threw up.

It was difficult to find food to make up for the lack of bread. Game was still scarce, and domestic stock was still very limited. There were few milk cows and little milk for the children. The families were also restricted in the

35. Hildreth, *Pioneer History*, 245; "Joseph Barker's Journal," in *The Ohio Frontier: An Anthology of Early Writings*, ed. Emily Foster (Lexington: University Press of Kentucky, 1996), 90–92.
36. May, *Journals*, 122–23; Hildreth, *Pioneer History*, 349–53, 419–22.

use they could make of the sugar maples in the area, because there was a shortage of kettles needed to boil the sap.

More difficult to understand is the inability of the settlers to avoid their worst food shortages by fishing. Early residents of the region often commented on the huge fish, particularly catfish and pike, that could be pulled from the Ohio and its tributaries, and fish were taken both on hooks and by spearing. Yet, while some families had fish, the rivers did little to ease the general shortage of food. Samuel Hildreth, the early chronicler of the region, argued that only a few of these New England settlers were skilled fishermen. Another major difficulty with making use of fish, except in the coldest months, was the acute shortage of salt. In the spring and summer any good catch of fish had to be eaten promptly. It was often not possible to save it by salting, and smokehouses were not typical of these settlements.

In the early years, nearly all the salt used in the Ohio Company settlements was brought across the Alleghenies on packhorses. It was very scarce and expensive. Even if there had been more hogs, and as yet there were very few, the settlers did not have the salt to preserve the pork.

One notable element in the time of crisis in the spring and early summer of 1790 was the generosity of settlers who shared with their neighbors. A few settlers with money had been able to buy provisions in the previous summer from traders who brought boats down the Ohio from western Pennsylvania. By May 1790, when some families were in danger of starvation, those with supplies proved willing to share what little they had. Also, the Ohio Company settlers benefited from the generosity of backwoodsman Isaac Williams, who for several years had lived across the Ohio River from Muskingum in what then was in the far western region of Virginia. He had been able to plant early enough in 1789 to avoid the killing frost and had several hundred bushels of good corn. Speculators offered to buy it from him at an inflated price, but he refused the offer. He sold it directly to Ohio Company settlers at the usual price and gave credit to those who had no money.

By the end of the winter, many of the poorest families were completely out of cornmeal. Some had a few potatoes stored from the previous year, but it was said that even in one of the more substantial families, where the man of the house had been an army major, the smaller children were reduced first to one potato a day, and then to half a potato. In cabins where there were young male lodgers, who kept their own small supplies of food, children were sent out of the cabin while a lodger's corn was cooked by the mother. As spring came, the pioneers turned to the plants in the woods to ease their hunger pangs. First available were nettles, but purslane was the most important, and when possible it was boiled with a tiny piece of venison and a dash of salt. Some families, however, had no meat to use with it.

What became known to these Ohio settlers as "the starving year" came to an end in July 1790 when new corn was in the milk. Beans and squash also became available. Soup was made from the corn and beans, before either had fully matured. Fortunately 1790 was a bumper year for crops. Meat continued to be scarce throughout the summer, but in the fall great swarms of turkeys landed in the midst of the settlements and were slaughtered with ease. Game returned to the vicinity, and the worst food shortage was over.[37]

For the next few years, the main difficulty in providing food was the danger involved in farming and hunting. The Indian tribes south of the Great Lakes were making their last strong effort to protect their homes in the region from the rapidly encroaching frontiersmen. From early in 1791, the Marietta region was under siege. Outlying settlements that had been established in the summer of 1790 were abandoned, and settlers gathered at Marietta, Belpre, and Waterford. At each of these places, blockhouses were built, and settlers left their cabins to live within the palisades surrounding the blockhouses.

Providing food entailed constant danger. At Belpre, where some of the farm clearings around abandoned cabins were three miles from "Farmers' Castle" (the main blockhouse), they had to be visited by fifteen or twenty men; some stood guard at the edge of the forest while others worked. The trip there became so dangerous that two more fortifications were built closer to the outlying fields. Although game had returned, the state of siege meant that meat was often in short supply as hunting was very dangerous. In the fall of 1791, one of the two backwoodsmen who hunted for the Belpre settlers was killed three miles from the garrison.[38]

In spite of all the difficulties, the Ohio Company settlers were never again so desperate for food as they had been in the spring and early summer of 1790. When missionary John Heckewelder visited Marietta in June 1792 he described the dangers, but he also emphasized the success that had been achieved in farming. There were now thousands of fruit trees, vegetable gardens, and even a few vineyards. In spite of all the hardships, the settlers had farmed so successfully that they had been able to sell

37. Hildreth, *Pioneer History,* 264–66, 351–59, 401–2, 405; Cutler, *Life of Ephraim Cutler,* 276.
38. Hildreth, *Pioneer History,* 275–303, 360–99; Cutler, *Life of Ephraim Cutler,* 24–27.

surpluses of ten thousand bushels of corn and four thousand pounds of bacon to the army contractor. The Ohio Company settlers no longer lacked their basic corn and salt pork.[39]

The early experiences of the Ohio Company pioneers were paralleled in many ways by the experiences of those who went farther down the Ohio River to settle in the region of Cincinnati on a large area of land bought by Judge John Cleves Symmes. The first settlements were made in the late fall of 1788. In the first winter, the settlers made up for their lack of corn by hunting and by eating various roots, but the situation deteriorated rapidly.

A pioneer who arrived at Columbia in 1789 later reminisced about the near-famine conditions of his first winter and spring. Early frost in the fall of 1789 killed the corn, and Indian attacks prevented hunters from bringing in meat. The two hundred or so settlers in Columbia lived on small amounts of poor corn, ground by hand, or boiled whole, and roots of bear grass, which were boiled, mashed up, and baked. Symmes complained that the government had left his three villages practically defenseless and that many settlers were leaving. He said some in Kentucky called the Miami Purchase the "Slaughterhouse."

The Miami settlements remained extremely dangerous until the mid-1790s, but the food situation gradually improved. In the spring of 1790, Symmes estimated that the Miami settlements would be able to plant about a thousand acres of corn. This was almost certainly an overly optimistic estimate because Symmes was anxious to retain the settlers he had and to convince new settlers to come. Settlers had felt particularly threatened since November 1791, when the Indians had routed an army led by Gen. Arthur St. Clair, but a benefit from that overwhelming defeat was that the army needed less beef. This meant that bullocks could be sold to the settlers to be gelded as oxen. The settlers needed them to pull the plows that would enable them to provide more corn. Over half the inhabitants had been raising corn by using hoes rather than plows. To help ease the situation, Symmes bought a dozen bullocks and rented them out to settlers who could not afford to buy them.[40]

In July 1792, missionary John Heckewelder described Cincinnati as a

39. Heckewelder, *Thirty Thousand Miles*, 261–65; Hildreth, *Pioneer History*, 473.

40. John Cleves Symmes, *The Correspondence of John Cleves Symmes: Founder of the Miami Purchase*, ed. Beverley W. Bond (New York: Macmillan, 1926), 94, 125–28, 156–57; Charles Gist, *The Cincinnati Miscellany, 1792–1868*, 2 vols. (1845–1846; repr., New York: Arno Press, 1971), 2:147–48; letter of Luke Foster, in Foster, ed. *Ohio Frontier*, 80–81; Oliver M. Spencer, *The Indian Captivity of O. M. Spencer*, ed. Milo M. Quaife (1835; repr., Chicago: R. R. Donnelley, 1917), 35–36.

settlement of nearly a thousand people, growing corn, wheat, oats, barley, millet, potatoes, and turnips. Fort Washington, the military post there, had a garrison of some two hundred men and "very fine large gardens" with vegetables and beautiful flowers. Farther down the river, he passed other settlements and was able to buy butter and watermelons. This, however, was still a very sparsely settled area, and there were also "great numbers of wild turkeys and geese."[41]

In 1797, in southwestern Ohio, British traveler Francis Baily commented that the inhabitants of the village of Columbia generally raised enough corn and cattle for their own needs but also bought many items from trading boats coming down the Ohio from western Pennsylvania. Fresh meat and vegetables were scarce in winter and spring, and the settlers depended a good deal on venison and wild turkey along with "bacon." For dinner, at the house of a doctor, he was given stewed pork with beef and "some wild sort of vegetable" gathered from the woods. For breakfast, at the home of a man who was a farmer and merchant as well as a preacher, Baily was given boiled chicken, buckwheat cakes, tea, and coffee. Buckwheat cakes were often eaten in the region. As he approached Columbia, Baily saw people everywhere tapping sugar maples. The settlers of southern Ohio had survived their most dangerous years.[42]

On the outer fringes of this first frontier across the Alleghenies not all the eating followed the typical pattern of the first settlers of Kentucky and Ohio. Along the trade routes of the Great Lakes—at Mackinac, Detroit, Green Bay, and Prairie du Chien—and as far as the Mississippi River, there was a scattering of small French settlements. These had been established by fur traders from French Canada. When Great Britain took Canada from France in 1763 these remained largely untouched, although some French crossed the Mississippi to settle in the region around St. Genevieve in what was then Spanish territory. It eventually became part of the United States as a result of the Louisiana Purchase.

These settlers existed precariously on a little fur trading, hunting, and on the products of their small farms, but their food and cooking reflected their distant French origins. Henry Brackenridge, who spent time with a family at St. Genevieve in the early 1790s, found the food very different from that in most American settlements. The interminable fried salt pork and cornmeal mushes of the Ohio valley were absent. The French Canadians

41. Heckewelder, *Thirty Thousand Miles*, 267–78.
42. Baily, *Journal*, 91, 92.

made much use of well-prepared vegetables, and soups, gumbos, and other prepared dishes replaced the constant frying or baking. They did not use tea, but the father of the family had coffee at breakfast.[43]

Elizabeth Baird, who was born in 1810 and spent her childhood on Mackinac Island, another French Canadian settlement, remembered sugar making on a nearby island where they had a dinner consisting of "partridges roasted on sticks before the fire; rabbit and stuffed squirrel, cooked French fashion; and finally had as many crêpes, with syrup, as we desired." On Christmas Eve, after a service lasting until midnight, they ate what "was considered the high feast of the season." She could no longer remember the entire menu but recalled roast pig, roast goose, chicken pie, round of beef, sausages, head cheese, *pattes d'ours* (chopped meat in a crust in the shape of bear's paws), souse, small fruit preserves, and small cakes.[44]

Visitors to Mackinac in the first decades of the nineteenth century were impressed both by the beauty of the island and by the abundance of fish. In 1820 Henry Schoolcraft saw canoeloads of fish—mainly trout and whitefish—being brought into market every morning. Ten years later, another visitor described "a lovely bay . . . dotted with canoes and the boats of the fishermen." Ojibwa and Ottawa Indians came to the island in great numbers to trade furs and to sell maple sugar, corn, beans, wild rice, and a variety of items made by the Indian women.[45]

While the tiny French settlements of the Old Northwest long remained isolated from the steady advance of American settlement, many pioneers had the opportunity to see French and Spanish influence on the lower reaches of the Mississippi. The pioneers who crossed the Alleghenies found that it was too difficult and expensive to ship their bulk farm produce back eastward over the mountains for sale. The only practical route was by flatboat or barge down the Ohio-Mississippi River system to the settlements on the lower Mississippi. New Orleans, which had come to the United States as part of the Louisiana Purchase in 1803, had a way of life and food that reflected its French and Spanish past.

For the most part, the long journey south on the Mississippi was through sparsely settled or unsettled areas. After passing Louisville, a traveler would not see another main town until Natchez in pioneer Mississippi Territory.

43. Henry M. Brackenridge, *Recollections of People and Places in the West* (Philadelphia, 1834), 25.

44. Elizabeth Thérèse Baird, "Reminiscences of Early Days on Mackinac Island," *Collections of the State Historical Society of Wisconsin* (Madison, 1888–1911), 14:21, 32–35.

45. Henry R. Schoolcraft, *Summary Narrative of an Exploratory Expedition to the Sources of the Mississippi River in 1820* (Philadelphia, 1855), 69–71; Juliette Kinzie, *Wau-Bun: The "Early Day" in the North-West*, intro. Milo M. Quaife (1856; repr., Chicago: R. R. Donnelley, 1932), 5, 7–8.

In 1800 it had a population of under five thousand. It was a raucous little place that catered to the boatmen with bars and brothels. In 1797 its surrounding region was described by English traveler Francis Baily as "not very forward in the luxuries or even the conveniences of life." The "plantations" he described were poor farms with a few slaves. Traveling in the area, he was usually given "a mess of *mush* and milk, some fried bacon, or some fresh meat of any kind."[46]

About ten years later, Fortescue Cuming, another British traveler, received "a tolerably good supper" at a tavern when he was traveling from Natchez to West Florida. It consisted of sliced bacon, bread and butter, and "a fine dish of gaspar-goo, the best fish I had yet tasted of the produce of the Mississippi." Gaspergoo is a lean, good-tasting freshwater fish found in deep waters in many places in the United States. At that time it was said that the market in Natchez was well known for its fish. The beef was poor. The farmers around Natchez used most of their land for cotton and depended on the boats coming down the river for their provisions.[47]

Mississippi Territory was still in an early stage of settlement, but farther south, along the lower Mississippi in Louisiana, travelers arrived in a region that had long been settled by the French and Spanish. At an inn in the small town of Baton Rouge, Cuming found the table covered with different items, of which the most prominent was a large dish of gumbo. This, he said, was standard fare among the French of the region, but the recipe he gave was basic: okra boiled until it was tender and seasoned with a bit of fat bacon. Many cooks obviously did a great deal better with their gumbo.[48]

With a population of some ten thousand, of which over half were slaves or free blacks, New Orleans was the biggest town in the Mississippi valley in the early years of the nineteenth century. The levee was crowded with boats from the upper country, and in the town backwoodsmen found food and entertainment that was unavailable on the farms of the Ohio valley. Markets in the city were particularly rich in fish, and a profusion of fruit—oranges, lemons, melons, pineapples—as well as nuts were sold about the streets by the free blacks. The gumbo eaten in New Orleans was not the simple product described by Fortescue Cuming in Baton Rouge. A visitor to New Orleans in 1804 described gumbo as a dish made of all possible ingredients, especially shrimp, which was another favorite food of the locals.

46. Baily, *Journal*, 200.
47. "Cuming's Tour to the Western Country (1807–1809)," in *Early Western Travels*, 4:330; Ker, *Travels*, 42.
48. "Cuming's Tour," 339–40.

Two years later, another visitor found excellent food at the boardinghouses, with fish, soup, abundant vegetables, and a variety of roasted, boiled, and stewed meats, but there was much less milk than upriver, and butter was not readily available.[49]

The drinking water was unpalatable in New Orleans. All the water used in the city was carried from the river in casks. It was laden with silt, and when a half-pint glass of water was left to settle, it finished with a half-inch of sediment in the bottom. Many avoided the problem by drinking liquor. Abundant corn whiskey came down the river in barrels, and the locals made a drink known as "taffia" from sugarcane. Those with more money also drank a good deal of wine. In the 1780s and 1790s visitors who came from isolated or beleaguered farms in Ohio and Kentucky found another world in New Orleans.[50]

Daily life on the farms of the Ohio valley remained much the same for many decades, but times of scarcity were succeeded by an abundance of food. By 1810, Kentucky's population was over 400,000, and in the following year a traveler riding west out of Lexington was impressed by the "finely cultivated fields, rich gardens, and elegant mansions, principally of brick, all the way."[51]

Kentucky had slaves from its earliest years, and in 1811 English traveler John Melish commented that the slaves in Kentucky were generally as well fed as the whites, and that it appeared to him that "they were better fed, better lodged, and better clothed than many of the peasantry in Britain." Reality was far removed from that rosy picture, and Melish's comment is more revealing about the condition of many of the poor in England than that of the slaves in Kentucky. Years later Daniel Drake's comment about slavery in his early years in Kentucky was that "the treatment of negroes at that time was severe," and that in regard to food, punishment, and required service, their conditions had improved since that time.[52]

A traveler at an inn in Ohio in 1807 was given "good coffee, roast fowls, chicken pie, potatoes, bread and butter, and cucumbers both sliced and

49. Baily, *Journal*, 310; John F. Watson, "Notitia of Incidents at New Orleans in 1804 and 1805," in *The American Pioneer*, 2 vols. (Cincinnati, 1842–43), 2:228, 233; Thomas Ashe, *Travels in America Performed in 1806*, 3 vols. (London, 1808), 3:261–62.

50. Ker, *Travels*, 47; Schultz, *Travels*, 2:199–200; Samuel J. Mills and Daniel Smith, *Report of a Missionary Tour through That Part of the United States Which Lies West of the Allegany Mountains* (Andover, Mass., 1815), 43.

51. Melish, *Travels*, 2:183; Richard C. Wade, *The Urban Frontier: The Rise of Western Cities, 1790–1830* (Cambridge: Harvard University Press, 1959), 80.

52. Melish, *Travels*, 2:207; Drake, *Pioneer Life*, 206.

pickled, all not only good, but delicate and fine even to the pastry." Four years later, when John Melish traveled down the Ohio River, he commented that, twenty years before, a friend of his on the same route had hardly been able to find provisions; now the banks of the river were "studded with towns and farm-houses, so close, that I slept on shore every night." In June 1817 at the small town of Rushville, an English traveler sat down to a breakfast that consisted of "coffee, rolls, biscuits, dry toast, waffles (a soft hot cake of German extraction, covered with butter) pickerell salted (a fish from Lake Huron), veal cutlets, broiled ham, gooseberry pie, stewed currants, preserved cranberries, butter and cheese." The traveler complained of "discordant dishes." He could hardly complain of the quantity.[53]

By 1815 Cincinnati was a flourishing town. Its merchants bought farm produce from farms in the surrounding areas and sent large quantities of flour, salt pork, corn whiskey, peach brandy, cheese, and all types of provisions to settlements along the lower Mississippi. There were four markets a week. There were ample supplies of beef, veal, pork, mutton, and poultry along with venison, fish, and, occasionally, bear meat. Butter and cheese came in from the surrounding farms, as did an abundance of vegetables and fruits: apples, pears, peaches, cherries, plums, strawberries, and melons.[54]

The advance through the great forests east of the Mississippi was temporarily slowed by the War of 1812, which brought fighting both south of the Great Lakes and on the Gulf of Mexico and a temporary renewal of Indian resistance, but the full flow of settlement renewed with ever-increasing force after the war. While some pioneers moved farther north or took less desirable lands in already settled areas, others advanced onto the prairies, a great expanse of land that stretched westward from Illinois across the Mississippi to the Great Plains.

53. "Cuming's Tour," 221; Melish, *Travels*, 2:147; Morris Birkbeck, *Notes on a Journey in America* (1818; repr., Ann Arbor: University Microfilms, 1966), 64.
54. Drake, *Natural and Statistical View*, 140–42, 148–49.

CHAPTER 2

# Land of Pork and Corn

Mutton is almost as abhorrent to an American palate, or fancy, as the flesh of swine to an Israelite.

Englishman Morris Birkbeck, 1822

 When settlers began to move out of the eastern forests onto the prairies, for the most part they were able to retain their old patterns of eating. The prairie region was generally well watered, and there were trees along the rivers and around the lakes. Away from the rivers, areas of woodland were interspersed with extensive stretches of land that were covered with grasses that often grew above head height. Most of the early pioneers sought out the wooded areas. This was what they knew, and they believed that trees meant fertility. Even if settlers were tempted onto the prairies by the prospect of avoiding the heavy labor of clearing the land, they discovered that the matted grass roots made plowing an extremely difficult process. A heavier plow was needed than had been used in the woodlands to the east, and a strong team of oxen was required to pull it. The prairies often remained unplowed until there was more settlement and greater prosperity.[1]

The diet of Americans in the prairie regions, as it appeared to others, can be seen through the eyes of a group of comparatively prosperous English immigrants who came directly from England to settle what became known as the "English Prairie" in southeastern Illinois. In 1817 Morris Birkbeck and George Flower bought lands in a region some fifty miles north of Shawneetown and encouraged other Englishmen to join them.

---

1. See John Mack Faragher, *Sugar Creek: Life on the Illinois Prairie* (New Haven: Yale University Press, 1986), 10–11.

American pioneers had already begun to move into the area, many of them from southern states—Kentucky, Tennessee, or North Carolina. Their lives fascinated the English.[2]

These first Americans in the area depended heavily on game, pork, and corn, although as settlement increased more began to plant beans, turnips, shallots, radishes, cucumbers, and cabbages. Morris Birkbeck said his American neighbors depended mainly on hogs for their food, but that they held bear meat in high esteem. Bears were numerous and were usually hunted in winter after they had fattened on hickory nuts and other mast.

John Woods, a newly arrived English farmer, thought that his American neighbors spent much of their time hunting and that they drank a great deal of whiskey. He was particularly struck by the American habit of using all sorts of occasions for a "Frolic." Corn husking, clearing logs and underbrush, cabin and barn raisings, and reaping were all occasions to gather the neighbors to work, drink, and eat. The women had sewing and quilting frolics, and whiskey circulated on these occasions, as it did when the men gathered.

Many of these southerners had added smokehouses to their log cabins, and they hung their bacon above slow-burning fires. They left it there longer than was usual in England because the warmer American summers meant the bacon had to be particularly well dried. For Woods's taste, the Americans did not use enough salt. This cautious use of salt reflected the salt shortages typical of life on the edge of the American frontier.[3]

The English settlers soon had to make use of salt pork, but they found it difficult to understand the extent to which it dominated the American frontier diet. The English had brought their love of mutton and lamb with them to America, and they were puzzled that Americans held mutton "in the utmost contempt" and said that people who ate it belonged to the family of wolves. Woods claimed that when "bacon" from the hogs slaughtered at the beginning of winter was exhausted, many Americans would live on corn bread for a month "rather than eat an ounce of mutton, veal, rabbit, goose, or duck." This was an obvious exaggeration, as he could have found many frontiersmen who ate rabbits and duck, but his main point about a diet dominated by salt pork accurately represented frontier tastes.

2. See Charles Boewe, *Prairie Albion: An English Settlement in Pionee Illinois* (Carbondale: Southern Illinois University Press, 1962); Morris Birkbeck, *Letters from Illinois* (London, 1818); Morris Birkbeck, *Notes on a Journey in America* (1818; repr., Ann Arbor: University Microfilms, 1966).

3. Woods, *Two Years Residence,* 129, 154–55, 159–61, 174; Birkbeck, *Notes,* 12, 141; George Flower, *The Errors of Emigrants* (1841; repr., New York: Arno Press, 1975), 22.

Morris Birkbeck reached the same conclusion. "Mutton," he wrote, "is al-most as abhorrent to an American palate, or fancy, as the flesh of swine to an Israelite." In Kentucky, he had heard, "even the negroes would no more eat mutton than they would horse-flesh."[4]

Farther north in Illinois, along Sugar Creek, in what became Sangamon County, Illinois, the first settlers were not "backwoodsmen" in the sense of many of those Americans in the area of the English Prairie, but, like back-woodsmen, they avoided the actual prairies, except, in the settlers' case, for grazing their cattle. John Mack Faragher has given a detailed description of their life. The settlers built their cabins and farmed in woods along the creek. As they came in to make their first clearings, they brought provisions and cows with them and supplemented their corn bread and milk by hunt-ing game and searching for wild honey. The area was particularly rich in hives. Their food was very much like that of the earlier settlers along the Ohio.

The heavier plows needed for prairie grasslands did not generally be-come available in the region until the late 1830s and 1840s, and until then the prairies around Sugar Creek remained unplowed. Sugar Creek settlers chopped down trees, planted corn among the stumps, and, before there were water mills, used horse-powered mills to grind their grain. In the fall, after the crop was in, they hunted. Much of the game rapidly diminished in numbers, but deer remained numerous into the 1840s, and squirrels and rabbits increased as they fed on growing crops. All three were eaten. Be-fore the settlers dug wells, they gathered water in troughs from the eaves and took water from the creek.

By 1840, the Sangamon settlers were well established. The typical farm grew mostly corn and a small amount of wheat. They had hogs, cattle, oxen, milk cows, poultry, and, more surprisingly, a few sheep. They had gardens for vegetables and peach or apple trees. Farm wives produced extra butter and eggs to sell in town. They also made good use of the many bee-hives and the abundant sugar maples, but corn, pork, and game remained at the heart of their diet in the early years.[5]

The English immigrants who settled on the English Prairie, like many other nationalities who came to the American frontier, hoped they could live and eat as the prosperous in their homeland lived and ate. They quickly found, however, that though their resources made their lives easier than those of many pioneer Americans, the American environment quickly

4. Woods, *Two Years Residence*, 134–36; Birkbeck, *Notes*, 83–84.
5. Faragher, *Sugar Creek*, 3–104.

reshaped their patterns of farming and eating. Unlike the first American settlers, these English immigrants wanted to cultivate the prairies. They viewed it as an advantage that they had found an area with numerous large "meadows" that allowed plowing and planting without extensive clearing.[6]

When Morris Birkbeck made the first settlement in 1817, he built his cabin just within the woods at the very edge of the prairie. He had good luck in hunting. In January 1818, he wrote that for the past month he had not sat down to dinner without a fine roast turkey. Wild turkeys were still numerous throughout the area. He also enjoyed wild grapes, said there were gooseberries and currants "in perfection," but thought the crab apples were inferior in size and flavor to the English variety.[7]

Other English immigrants joined Birkbeck in the summer of 1818. The first two parties combined numbered fewer than one hundred. At first, they lived in small log cabins provided by Birkbeck, and for food they fell back on the Ohio valley staples of corn bread and salt pork. Most of them found corn bread rather unpalatable. Indian corn (which in England was called maize) had spread to Europe after the Europeans had reached the Americas, but it had not become as popular there as it was in the United States. In England, growers used it to feed their livestock. Unlike the Americans, who planted corn as quickly as possible, the English in southern Illinois planted very little when they first arrived. In the following year, they put in wheat and other grains along with corn. This delay was possible because most of them were relatively prosperous.[8]

In the summer of 1818, the English survived by buying provisions from the settlement of New Harmony in southern Indiana as well as game from the American backwoodsmen already settled in the region. Even with money, the English experienced some food shortages. On one day George Flower's family was reduced to eating the tenderest buds and shoots of a hazel tree. The English also had difficulty finding water. The water level in the area was low, and the first efforts to dig wells, even when settlers went to a considerable depth, often failed.[9]

When John Woods came to the settlement in the fall of 1819, he had the money to buy provisions and a cast iron stove at Shawneetown on the Ohio. He had heard it would be difficult to obtain a stove on the prairies.

6. In his book *Revolution in Eating*, James E. McWilliams discusses how, in colonial America, the English in different regions had different levels of success in recreating patterns of diet known in England.

7. Birkbeck, *Letters*, 30–31, 39–40.

8. Woods, *Two Years Residence*, xix–xx, 153; Birkbeck, *Letters*, 43–44.

9. Boewe, *English Prairie*, 83–84, 87, 91, 116, 133; Woods, *Two Years Residence*, 12–22; Milo M. Quaife, ed., *Pictures of Illinois: One Hundred Years Ago* (Chicago: R. R. Donnelley, 1918), 46.

It was a rare item among settlers in the first decades of the nineteenth century. Practically all the pioneers cooked over an open fire within their cabins. Much of the food was fried in a skillet placed in the embers or boiled in an iron pot hung over the flames. Often the skillet was a spider—a pan with legs and a lid.

By the time Woods reached the prairies, the first main year of English cultivation was nearly over, and there were now some four hundred English and seven hundred Americans in the vicinity of the English Prairie. As he had money, Woods was able to take advantage of improvements made by the first settlers. He bought a farm with growing crops of Indian corn, pumpkins, beans, and shallots (which Americans in the area preferred to onions), three cows, three calves, three sheep, more than thirty hogs, and "a considerable deal" of poultry. Hogs soon predominated in the English settlements as well as in the American.[10]

Woods, like earlier settlers, had difficulty obtaining enough water. He had two wells dug, but one gave no water and the other very little. He finally had luck with a third. The poorly producing well was used as a place to put fresh meat, as it proved to be the best place to keep off the flies. The meat was lowered in a bucket. Some items that had been staples in England were scarce. Butter was not yet plentiful, there was little cheese, and Woods missed beer and cider. Butter, cheese, and beer quickly became more readily available. Morris Birkbeck established a dairy herd of twenty cows with the specific object of making cheese.[11]

The English settlers were far more anxious than the Americans to plant a wheat crop. Some of them never developed a taste for corn bread, but they made extensive use of corn as a winter feed for their stock and learned to accept it in various boiled forms. Surprisingly, the English were at first reluctant to eat corn on the cob. In accounts of the settlements they wrote for English audiences, they found it necessary to explain that the Americans used corn as a vegetable. Pumpkins, also unknown in England, were far more acceptable. The immigrants quickly learned to use them in pies and to make sauces. Woods thought the sauce was good and the pies excellent. Pumpkins were also sliced and dried for winter use.[12]

The English quickly took advantage of the natural food resources that America provided. Woods thought that the fruits in the surrounding woods and prairies varied from "excellent" to "indifferent." When he had first traveled into the region from the Ohio River, he had found hazelnuts in "vast

10. Woods, *Two Years Residence*, xv–xvi, 97, 106–7.
11. Ibid., 121–22, 133, 207.
12. Ibid., 152, 155.

quantities." He did not particularly like the wild grapes he found, but some that had nearly dried to raisins made good eating in sauces and in tarts. Wild strawberries, blackberries, and elderberries were all excellent. The raspberries were small and dry, the wild plums small and sour, but the wild May apples were better. He also sampled a pawpaw and obtained honey from beehives in the woods.[13]

Some of the English went out on bear and deer hunts, but Woods made most use of the small game, which was the only game available to most farmers in England. American rabbits had darker flesh than those he had been used to in England, but they were more moist and tender. Prairie chickens, which Woods described for English readers as a kind of grouse (they are closely related), were "extremely palatable," and the quail (which he said were called partridges in America) were "uncommonly fine flavoured."[14]

The three daily meals described by Woods as typical reflect the degree to which the English, while retaining some of their own food preferences, were obliged by the nature of the country, the crops, and the livestock to eat in a manner familiar to Americans. The typical breakfast was bacon, beef, eggs, butter, honey, bread, and tea or coffee. Dinner (at the modern lunchtime) was "some sort of pudding," with meat or game, and water to drink, and supper the same as breakfast. Salt pork quickly became a staple in the English diet, although they added beef when they could.[15]

Woods found that many of the herbs that he had known in England, or different varieties of them, were available in the new settlements. Among those that he mentioned were fennel, sage, parsley, balm, pennyroyal, and horehound. The last three are all varieties of mint. Pennyroyal (or pudding grass) and horehound were sometimes used to make tea. Horehound mixed with molasses was also given to children with colds. The sage Woods encountered was different than that in England. Peppermint and spearmint were scarce, and Woods did not see any thyme.[16]

By the summer of 1821, Woods was well established. He had wheat, corn, oats, barley, peas, potatoes, and a variety of garden vegetables. There was now plenty of cheese being produced in the settlement, and Woods was able to obtain beer. An Englishman at Wanborough was brewing a large amount. As he had no barley, he was making his malt from wheat, presumably producing a type of German "weiss" beer. Venison and other

13. Ibid., 102, 162–64, 215.
14. Ibid., 141–42; Birkbeck, *Letters from Illinois,* 40.
15. Woods, *Two Years Residence,* 200.
16. Ibid., 158.

game were not as plentiful as in the previous year, but wild fruits were readily available. As early as 1822, the English Prairie residents were able to send corn, flour, pork, and beef downriver to New Orleans.[17]

Most immigrants to Illinois were not as well organized and prosperous as those who settled on the English Prairie, and light is thrown on the life of a more marginal English immigrant family in the story of Rebecca Burlend. In 1831, Mrs. Burlend left her leased farm near a small village in Yorkshire to come with her husband and five of her children to settle in Pike County, Illinois. The Burlends were better off than most immigrants in that they had enough money to invest in a farm in America, but the investment took much of their savings. They were not in a position to take advantage of the fertile prairies. In raising food their problem was not the lack of the right type of plow to tackle the tangled roots; it was the lack of any plow at all.

When the Burlends left their tiny village to travel to Illinois they had never been more than forty miles from home. They sailed steerage class from Liverpool to New Orleans, went by steamboat up the Mississippi to St. Louis, and then took another steamboat to Phillip's Ferry on the Illinois River, only two miles from where they intended to settle. They landed on a November evening, and there was not a person or a building in sight. A forest pressed down to the edge of the river. While her husband trudged into the woods to try to find where to go, Rebecca and her five children sat alone in the darkness over four thousand miles from home.[18]

Mr. Burlend found a cabin where the occupants agreed they could lodge for a few days if they paid and provided their own provisions. Many pioneers greeted newcomers more warmly. In the three days they spent in that first cabin, Mrs. Burlend had her first glimpse of the food they would eat in America. Dangling from the ceiling of the cabin were two or three pieces of bacon, smoked till until they were almost black, and some pieces of beef. In the cellar were two or three large tubs of lard, and under a bed were three or four large jars of honey. The American family used the honey at every meal as well as coffee.

The Burlends were not asked to share in the food, though their children were offered the liquid in which cabbage had been cooked. Mrs. Burlend suggested that her children were used to better. She was quite surprised that this frontier housewife liked to smoke—it was probably a corncob pipe, a common item on the frontier. Based on her experience in Pike

17. Ibid., 219–21; Quaife, ed., *Pictures of Illinois,* 47.

18. [Rebecca Burlend], *A True Picture of Emigration: or Fourteen Years in the Interior of North America,* ed. Milo M. Quaife (1848; repr., Chicago: Lakeside Press, 1936), vii–xxii, 43.

County over the next fifteen years, Mrs. Burlend concluded that Americans, in general, but particularly the women, were fond of smoking.[19]

From an earlier settler, the Burlends bought eighty acres of "improved" land. This left them with just enough money to get started. Twelve acres of the land had been broken, and three acres of wheat had been planted to grow over the winter, plus there was already a log cabin on the property. They were settling in the woods, not on the prairies. Mrs. Burlend described the "thousands of acres" of Illinois prairies, but said that they had to be broken with a prairie plow.[20]

The Burlends had brought supplies with them from England, and they had bought more in New Orleans, but those were now nearly gone, and they had to use some of their remaining money to buy a bushel of ground corn. They would have preferred wheat flour, but corn was one-third the price of wheat. As they had no oven and no yeast, Mrs. Burlend had to make a "sad paste" and "bake" the corn bread in a frying pan on hot ashes. That first winter they were able to get a little milk from their nearest neighbor, who lived about half a mile away. It generally had lumps of ice in it. For their first weeks in Illinois, their meals were usually "hasty pudding, sad bread, and a little venison." Hasty pudding was simply cornmeal mush sweetened with honey or molasses. They bought the venison from the man who had improved their land.

Practically the last of their money was used to buy a cow, a calf, two pigs, and a pan to bake in. This was a "shallow flat-bottomed iron pan, with a cover to it," which Mrs. Burlend said was commonly called "a skellit." To bake, she apparently used it like a Dutch oven—putting it in the embers of the fire to heat, removing it to put in dough, replacing the lid, returning it to the embers and throwing ashes and embers on top of it as well. A Dutch oven was a large cast-iron pot made with short legs so that it could be put directly into the embers of a fire. The tight-fitting lid had a raised rim so that coals could be placed on top. It was usually the only type of oven available to most early settlers.

In this part of Illinois the settlers did not bake a quantity of bread in advance as they did in England, but the bread was very good because eggs and milk were plentiful. For leavening they used "saleratus," a pioneer standby consisting mainly of potassium. This was used before more elaborate baking powders became available in the mid-nineteenth century.

The two pigs the Burlends had bought were soon killed to conserve the

19. Ibid., 43–46.
20. Ibid., 53–56.

family's small amount of corn. As English immigrants, the Burlends apparently did not know, or did not believe, that the pigs could fend for themselves in the woods. It was not the way that pigs were kept in Yorkshire. They were also unsure whether they could make use of land they did not own. In England, laws governing private land were very strict, and common land was very limited.

As the Burlends settled in for their first winter, that of 1831–1832, they lived modestly. They had plenty of corn bread and milk, but they missed beer and tea. Coffee was their main drink, but they carefully husbanded it. They had to thaw any water they wanted. They had little meat. They caught a few quail in snares and found them excellent eating. Mr. Burlend shot a few rabbits but was unable to kill any of the deer he saw because he did not have a rifle.

To raise money, the Burlends began to tap their sugar maples—they had about four hundred of them. Most of the syrup and sugar they made they bartered with a storekeeper who had provided them with a little corn meal on credit. In return they received Indian corn for seed, some cornmeal for their own use, a little coffee, two or three hoes, and a "Yankee axe," which was larger than an English axe.[21]

It was now March 1832, and the Burlends needed to plant their corn. As they had no plow and no team, they had to use hoes. It took them three weeks to prepare about four acres, which they sowed with corn and some potatoes. When the wheat planted by the previous owner came up, they exchanged it with the storekeeper for a plow, two tin milk bowls, and a few pounds of coffee. Later they bought three pigs. As the summer went on, more difficulties arose. The delay caused by their difficulties in breaking the soil with hoes—made worse by their inexperience with American conditions—meant that their corn was still green when it was ripe in other clearings in the neighborhood. They cut what little was ready. Also, for several weeks they had practically no meat. To get a few fowl they traded one of the teacups they had brought from England. To add to their irritations, they were plagued with mosquitoes, a constant summer complaint of settlers and explorers all the way across America.[22]

The Burlends, however, were beginning to appreciate some aspects of American frontier living. They had turned their meager stock out in the spring; Mrs. Burlend happily reported that in America, unlike England, all unenclosed land was considered common pasture. They were also learning

21. Ibid., 58–60, 71–79.
22. Ibid., 79–89, 107–9.

to use what the forest gave them. Nuts were plentiful. There were hazelnuts, filberts, and two kinds of walnuts. In their first years of settlement the
children gathered bushels of them. They also found that grapes, strawberries, and raspberries grew "wild in great abundance," and there were many
wild plum trees. The raspberries were much blacker when ripe than the
ones they were used to in England, but the flavor was much the same. Settlers in the area made wine from many of the berries.[23]

Problems with the corn were somewhat compensated for by a bumper
crop of potatoes, but the Burlends now had to cope with planting their
wheat. After their problems preparing the land for corn, they were reluctant to use hoes. The difficulty was solved by exchanging Mr. Burlend's
watch for eight acres of plowing and harrowing. This meant they could
sow more wheat, and in the following winter and spring their life became
a little better. They were again successful in tapping the sugar maples, and
they made some three hundred and fifty pounds of sugar. Forty pounds of
this was exchanged for a sow and a litter of pigs. They now had two milk
cows, two steers almost ready to be yoked, a young heifer, a calf (the cow
had calved again), and a mare. But they still had no team to plow, and it
was time to put in the corn. This time they were helped out by a neighbor
who plowed for them. Neighbors also gave them the seeds and plants
needed to start a garden. In the spring of 1833 Mr. Burlend prepared about
a quarter acre. It was planted mainly with potatoes but also with various
other vegetables. The worst was over. The Burlends gradually were making a success of their great adventure.[24]

Mrs. Burlend noted some distinct differences in the eating patterns of
the American pioneers of Pike County and the rural English. She found
a monotony in the three meals that the Americans ate every day. Corn
bread, butter, coffee, and "bacon" were always on the table, and, apart from
game, fresh meat was a rarity. In England, villagers went to the butcher
for fresh meat, but here in America, the farmers killed all their own livestock and salted most of what was not immediately eaten. Sometimes
pieces were sent to neighbors, who returned the favor when they killed
some of their own stock. Those who were well established fared better. It
was not unusual, she said, for "an old settler . . . to have a couple of fowl,
ducks, a goose, or a [wild] turkey to dinner," and in general "everybody has
plenty of plain good food."

Much of an American settler's time was devoted to the growth and

23. Ibid., 75–76, 95–96.
24. Ibid., 110–111, 113, 120–23.

management of the corn crop, which they often mingled with beans, melons, and pumpkins, to make use of the strong support provided by the corn stalks. The much hotter summers in Illinois, compared to England, meant that the melons and pumpkins, along with cucumbers and peaches, ripened early. Turnips were usually sown in July after the wheat was reaped, often on the wheat land itself. In winter the farmers fed their stock on corn. At the end of the year, after the leaves fell, farmers slaughtered the hogs and the horned cattle they did not want to keep over the winter. After the hogs were brought in from their feeding on the fallen nuts in the forest, they were usually given corn for a few weeks to improve the bacon. Food along the Illinois River in western Illinois in the 1830s differed little from food along the Muskingum in eastern Ohio thirty years before.[25]

By the late 1830s a steady stream of pioneers was beginning to move even farther west onto the prairie lands of what was to become the state of Iowa. In October 1839, newly married Kitturah Belknap and her husband left Ohio in a wagon pulled by two horses. Among their possessions were a Dutch oven, a skillet, a tea kettle, and a coffee pot. Each night they camped, cooked their supper, and slept in the wagon. As soon as they camped, and before she cooked, Mrs. Belknap began to make "salt rising" bread for the next day, putting her "rising" on "the warm ground" (presumably near the fire). The "rising" was the substitute for yeast. The next morning, Mrs. Belknap would add it to dough, make loaves, and bake them in the Dutch oven before the couple went on their way.

Salt rising is a leavened, tight-textured, flavorful bread, which was popular in the first half of the nineteenth century because it did not require yeast for fermentation. It can be made in various ways, but typically water, a little cornmeal, sliced potatoes, and salt are placed in a warm place overnight. The next day, the potatoes are removed, and the remaining liquid is used as leavening.

The Belknaps' route west took them through settled country, and they were able to stop at farmhouses to buy eggs, butter, cabbages, and feed for the horses. At Rushville, Illinois, they stopped for five weeks, thinking that they would remain there for the winter, but hearing of a land purchase from the Indians west of the Mississippi, they set out again in midwinter. They bought some cows to take with them and cooked provisions before they went. Near the Des Moines River they bought a land claim from a family of squatters, who had moved onto the land ahead of its sale, and

25. Ibid., 60–61, 130.

were able to trade with them for chickens and hogs. The farm was on the prairie, two miles from timber. They then set about farming, saving money to buy their land when the government put it on the market.

As the cultivation of prairie lands became more usual, a rough abundance of food usually arrived earlier in the settlement process. Less than two years after arriving, Mrs. Belknap was able to plan an elaborate Christmas dinner for twelve in her log cabin. There was to be a first course of roast spare ribs with sausage, mashed potatoes, and gravy, a second course of stewed chicken and gravy, as well as a chicken stuffed and roasted in a Dutch oven "by the fire." To go with the meat there was to be a sauce of dried apples, together with light rolls, and for dessert there was cake, doughnuts, and pumpkin pie, with crab apple and wild plum preserves. She thought she could "carry that out and have dinner by two o'clock if I get up early." This was all without a stove.[26]

Cooking without the use of a stove remained typical of pioneer settlements throughout the first decades of the nineteenth century. John Woods, the Englishman who took an iron stove from Shawnee town to the English Prairie in 1819, was representative of only a small minority of prosperous settlers. Sarah Welch, who settled with her family in Van Buren County, Iowa, in the late 1830s, was hired to cook with the owner's wife for forty-two men building mills. She was paid seventy-five cents a week. They had no stove and did all their cooking at the fireplaces.

In the early 1840s, Sarah married Wellington Nossaman. They moved farther into Iowa and settled "in the thick timber" on a claim near Pella in the central part of the state. In the first summer they lived in a shanty made of poles and covered with white elm bark. It had no fireplace. Mrs. Nossaman cooked outside on a log fire. When it rained they had no cooked food. In her reminiscences, she said it was before the time of stoves: "It was days of johnnycake boards, dutch ovens, skillets, and lids." To make johnnycake, she took a board eighteen by eight inches, with rounded corners and the edges thinner than the middle, spread it with corn dough, set it in front of a hot fire to bake one side "nice and brown," then turned it round to bake the other side.[27]

These early settlers continued to have problems in grinding their corn. In the fall of 1844 the Nossamans had good crops of corn and wheat, but the nearest mill was one hundred miles away. Mills were soon built much

26. "Diary of Kitturah Penton Belknap," in Glenda Riley, ed., *Prairie Voices: Iowa's Pioneering Women* (Ames: Iowa State University Press, 1996), 5–16.

27. Sarah Welch Nossaman and Mary Nossaman Todd, "Pioneering at Bonaparte and near Pella," in Riley, ed., *Prairie Voices*, 121–24.

closer, but in the meantime, they used a primitive mill powered by six oxen. It would grind about three pecks of corn an hour but no wheat. Mary Ann Davidson, who settled in Marshall County in the 1840s, recalled a great shortage of bread in the harsh winter of 1848–1849. Their only bread was made by pounding corn by hand. High water prevented them from crossing streams to reach the mill, and it was July before they had regular bread.[28]

Margaret Archer Murray, who as a child in the 1850s lived in Jones County, Iowa, later in her life recalled both what her mother and father had told her about their arrival in Iowa in 1846, as well as her own experiences. Cooking and food loomed large in these memories. Their log cabin had a very wide fireplace so that they could hang cooking vessels over the fire. These pots were all made of iron. Corn bread and mush and milk were staples, but other bread was made in a Dutch oven in the coals. When they first arrived, there was still ample game. Her father loved to hunt, and they had a great variety of meat: venison, wild turkey, prairie chicken, rabbit, and squirrel. He saw many buffalo, but never killed one. They kept cattle and sheep but never killed them for meat. In the fall they killed hogs and salted the meat in their pork barrel, and they kept and ate a lot of chickens.

Margaret wrote that her mother did not know how to can fruit and vegetables. She buried cabbages, turnips, beets, and potatoes to preserve them, made sauerkraut by the barrel, and put up pickles in salt. In summer she sold butter and eggs. The children gathered wild cherries, plums, chokecherries, crab apples, and blackberries. Some of these her mother dried to preserve. As spreads for their bread, they used honey, maple syrup, and pumpkin butter. Eventually they used dried pumpkin for pies, but they seldom had cakes or pies until they finally got a stove on the eve of the Civil War. In the early days it took Margaret Murray's parents a four-day round-trip to visit their nearest market.[29]

For decades after pioneers pressed on to the West Coast, settlers continued to move into Iowa. In 1858, Mary St. John came to Iowa from New York with her mother, brothers, and sisters to join her father, who had bought land on the prairie in the northeastern part of the state near the Minnesota border. She kept a diary, added to by others in the family, which described their daily life in the months after their arrival in April that year. They were settling in an area that had already been farmed by other settlers, and life was not as hard as for earlier pioneers.

28. Ibid., 124; Mary Ann Ferrin Davidson, "Autobiography," in Riley, ed., *Prairie Voices*, 35–36.
29. Margaret Archer Murray, "Memoir," in Riley, ed., *Prairie Voices*, 129–34.

The St. John family had a stove, and they immediately began to bake leavened bread, cakes, and pies. They still regularly ate johnnycake, but it was not eaten meal after meal, and leavened bread, pies, and custard puddings featured just as prominently in her journal. Soon after they arrived, the St. Johns were able to plant a garden and currant bushes. By August they were eating peas, beans, and new potatoes with their dinner. Like earlier settlers, they still gathered nuts and berries and hunted for ducks and pigeons, but hunting now provided special items rather than staples of their diet. The meat at their main meals in this first year was varied—chicken, freshly caught fish, beef, ducks, and pigeons. They apparently had not brought a pork barrel with them because bacon was not mentioned in their meals during most of the first year. This changed in December when they butchered two pigs. Salt pork was still essential in the winter.[30]

More variety was added to eating patterns in the eastern woodlands and prairies by the increasing number of immigrants. A whole kaleidoscope of other groups brought their own recipes and applied them to the familiar foods of the American pioneer. Norwegian Elisabeth Koren came to Washington prairie, southeast of Decorah in northeastern Iowa, late in 1853 as the young wife of a pastor coming to serve a Norwegian immigrant community. The area had been settled only four years earlier. During their first year, while a parsonage was readied for them, the Korens lived with one or another of their parishioners. Most of the three months after they arrived were spent in a cabin with a man, his wife, and two children. The cabin was fourteen by sixteen feet, divided into living and sleeping areas by a calico curtain. Another curtain divided the sleeping area.[31]

The Korens did not go hungry, but they found that typical Norwegian food had been much modified by pioneer conditions in the interior of North America. Elisabeth Koren missed both fish and soup, and she became extremely tired of salt pork. Within a few days of arriving, she complained in her journal that coffee took the place of soup. Later she was to say that in America there was coffee for breakfast, coffee instead of soup for dinner, and, "when things are really topsy-turvy, coffee for supper as well." At one dinner, a month after they arrived, she ate biscuits and drank coffee but declined the pork. Late in January, she was pleasantly surprised

30. Mary St. John, "Diary," in Riley, ed., *Prairie Voices*, 46–70.

31. [Elisabeth Koren], *The Diary of Elisabeth Koren, 1853–1855*, trans. and ed. David T. Nelson (Northfield, Minn.: Norwegian-American Historical Association, 1955), viii–xiii, 186–87.

when her hostess served a meat and vegetable soup. It had been a long time since she had tasted soup.[32]

They had arrived in winter, and Mrs. Koren soon realized that if she wanted meat it was salt pork or nothing. Early in February 1854 she described the meals they had been given in their first two months in Iowa: "The dishes vary from boiled pork to fried pork, rare to well done, with coffee in addition (milk when we can get it), good bread and butter. To this are added now and then potatoes, which are now all gone; fried onions, once in a while; and, above all, the glass jar of pickles. This is our meal morning, noon, and evening. But our appetites seldom fail." Even soup had its problems. One day she was glad she had already eaten when she watched her host and another man eating soup with pork and dumplings, "swimming in fat," carefully licking the backs of their spoons after each mouthful.[33]

The food situation was not quite as bleak as Elisabeth Koren painted it in her moments of frustration. Her complaints reflected her situation as a new bride living for a year with other families in tiny cabins, dependent on them for the food that was on the table. On special occasions these families made attempts to vary their food and to remember Norway. On their arrival in Iowa just before Christmas, the Korens spent three nights with the Katterruds and were given *flødegrød*, a Norwegian dish made by cooking thick sour cream with flour and milk. This was not regular fare for these Norwegian settlers. It had obviously been brought out to welcome the new pastor and his wife.

When the Korens moved in with Erik and Helene Egge to spend the first few months, Mrs. Egge brought out beer and "*fattigmandsbakkels*," or "poor-man's cake," a popular Norwegian pastry, to welcome them. *Fattigmand* was traditionally served with a glass of wine in the Christmas season. It is made from a dough of flour, eggs, cream, and sugar, cut into thin pieces, and fried in hot oil.[34]

On the day after Christmas, when they visited a neighbor, the Korens were first given *fattigmand* and a homemade grape wine, and for dinner there was "a table loaded with fried pork, spareribs, sausage, bread, butter, cakes, and excellent coffee." They stopped at another cabin for a taste of "Christmas beer" before arriving home to find supper set and Helene "waiting for us with her pork."[35]

32. Ibid., 134, 138.
33. Ibid., 156, 164.
34. Helen Myhre and Mona Vold, *Farm Recipes and Food Secrets from the Norske Nook* (New York: Crown Publishers, 1993), 254.
35. Koren, *Diary,* 99, 102, 104–6.

If the pastor and his wife arrived unexpectedly, things could be a little different. On a visit to one neighbor they found the table littered with potato peelings, meat bones, "and other remains of their breakfast." Anne Aarthun, the housewife, must have been shocked by the sudden arrival of the pastor, but she "soon brought some sort of order" and brought out "a glass of good beer and not-so-good cake." The Aarthuns obviously tried to redeem themselves, for within a week Helene Egge was able to serve roast quail, supplied by the Aarthuns, who later also brought a chicken and a jug of beer. Other gifts from neighbors included eggs, partridges, and a cheese, which was put in the cellar to age.[36]

In spring, for a month or two, the Korens moved in with a family where there was much more room and a housewife, Mrs. Koren noted, "who excels at setting a table with cakes and pies." There was still salt pork, but again it was varied by gifts. Veal was particularly welcome because it had been so long since they had tasted it. The Korens were still waiting for their parsonage, but in May they at last had a place of their own—a small cabin on an immigrant's farm. Young Mrs. Koren, who was now pregnant, began to keep house for her husband. They had a stove, but as it was too hot to have it in the one-room cabin, they had a small shed built for cooking.[37]

Mrs. Koren tried to make the dishes that had been familiar to her in Norway, particularly those which used dairy products. Favorites were *tykmelk,* a soup made with coagulated sour milk, and *flødegrød,* another dish with sour milk as a base. *Tykmelk* was a regular dish. One dinner consisted of egg pancakes and sour milk soup, with strawberries and cream to follow. She was lucky, Mrs. Koren wrote, to have a dish like sour milk soup in "this land of pork." In her efforts to serve Norwegian food, Mrs. Koren was much helped by the gifts they were given. They regularly received butter, eggs, cream, and flour, and, less often, cheese.[38]

When her husband was sick, Mrs. Koren went to considerable trouble to find barley to make him some barley soup. She managed to get some, ground it in her coffee mill, and made soup from it. For something to mix with it, she boiled some dried apples and used the juice, and served it with white bread and "rusks."[39]

Mrs. Koren was able to keep the dairy products she was given in a neighbor's "springhouse" built close to a small brook. During the early years of

36. Ibid., 122, 131–32, 169, 181.
37. Ibid., 189–90, 219, 224, 227.
38. Ibid., 228, 234–35, 241, 246, 250, 281, 294.
39. Ibid., 227–28.

settlement, keeping dairy products cool at the edge of a stream was very common. Mary Elizabeth Lyon, who settled in Iowa in the 1850s, remembered her mother putting milk and butter on a "shelving rock" tucked under the bank of a creek where there was a cool spring flowing. Keeping dairy products in summer was a particular problem because of the abundance of flies and the absence of screens. Matilda Paul, who went to Iowa as a child in the 1860s, remembered the flies "thick in the houses and all over everything." They waved a small tree branch thick with leaves to keep them off the food as they ate. They were also plagued by mosquitoes. Once they were better established, settlers might use mosquito netting at the doors and windows, or around the beds, but flies and mosquitoes were still a constant problem.[40]

The lack of fresh meat, and particularly the lack of fish, troubled Mrs. Koren. The locals still only butchered hogs, and there is no indication that they sent fresh pork to the Korens. Mrs. Koren wrote that the only way to get fresh meat was to kill a rooster or shoot a bird. Although there were abundant fish only three or four miles away, the Korens seldom had any, and they were delighted when a candidate for confirmation brought them "a fine mess of trout." In the following year, when Mrs. Koren was brought some fresh fish, she mentioned that it had been a year since she had tasted it. She longed for "some new potatoes and a little mackerel from home."[41]

Most of the fruit the Korens had in their first year in America was from the wild. In June strawberries were abundant, and they made extensive use of them. There were also many other fruits in the vicinity, including grapes, cherries, black currants, raspberries, and plums, as well as great numbers of hazelnuts. Watermelons, grown by some of their neighbors, were a special treat, and Mrs. Koren was delighted with her first taste.[42]

In the early fall of 1854 the Korens at last moved into their new parsonage, bringing with them fresh pork, carrots, beets, cabbage, and onions given to them by parishioners. They managed to find plates and knives in their luggage and sat down to bread, butter, and a brown Norwegian cheese—*mysost*. This is very much like the better-known *gjetost*, except that no goat's milk is mixed with the cow's milk. The gifts continued to flow in, testifying not only to the generosity of the parishioners but also to the extent that these new settlers had prospered in their new country. Among the food items the Korens received were a chicken, carrots, pota-

40. Ibid., 247; Mary Elizabeth Lyon, "Memories," in Riley, ed., *Prairie Voices*, 44; Matilda Peitzke Paul, "Memoirs," in Riley, ed., *Prairie Voices*, 164.
41. Koren, *Diary*, 228, 239, 361.
42. Ibid., 229, 234, 239, 259, 268, 285, 299–300.

toes, eggs, butter, prairie chickens, a leg of dried mutton, and venison (one batch was so salty that they could not eat it).[43]

In setting up a home for herself, and providing for the coming winter, Mrs. Koren had to turn to the salt pork she had objected to since arriving in the settlement. The Korens had arranged for a man to bring a hog for slaughter, and he turned up unexpectedly in mid-October when they had no barrel, no salt, and a cellar full of kindling. Neighbors helped by lending a barrel and salt and cutting up the meat. Space was cleared in the cellar, and in the following weeks two more hogs were brought and slaughtered. The third hog presented a problem because there was no barrel available. For a time after slaughtering it was simply left lying in the cellar until a barrel was ready for it.

With the killing of the first hog, Mrs. Koren seized on the chance to serve fresh meat—pork tenderloins. She also made her first headcheese by boiling down the hog's head into a jellied mass. This was seasoned and pressed into a mold. Mrs. Koren mentioned using almonds as one of her ingredients. Before her husband left on a trip, she served him a breakfast of fried chicken, headcheese, soft-boiled eggs, and coffee.

By the fall of 1855, when the church trustees ate at the parsonage, Mrs. Koren was able to serve a meal of "roast pork, of course, corn on the cob, pancakes, pickles, cucumbers, and sour milk soup." The process of transforming a Norwegian into an American diet was well under way.[44]

As settlers moved even farther west into Iowa, they had to get used to the absence of trees. In 1860, when May Crowder moved with her husband from Illinois to Iowa, they lived at first in a log cabin at the edge of the woods in Howard County, but in 1869 they moved to Palo Alto County. Here, they settled "in the middle of endless miles of prairie—not a tree or a shrub." Their first home was a little shanty made of two-by-fours and boards. It was built in a day. To build a proper home, they had to haul lumber from Fort Dodge, fifty miles way.

In November 1869, they moved into their house, and, though spartan, it reflected higher ambitions and opportunities than had been present in earlier years. They brought a stove from Fort Dodge, which they stoked with wood brought six miles from the Des Moines River. This meant they were often short of fuel both for cooking and for heat. Neighbors told them how to create substitutes for wood by twisting hay into tight bundles.

43. Ibid., 312–13, 320, 342, 350, 361.
44. Ibid., 321–22, 342, 344–45, 347, 351, 364.

There were still abundant natural resources. In their first fall, the Crowders went to the river with pails, sacks, and tubs to gather wild grapes, plums, and crabapples. Much of the fruit was preserved for the winter. Until they raised rhubarb, they occasionally gathered sheep sorrel and made pies of it. This was a little unusual. More typically sorrel leaves were used in soups or as potherbs. Sorrel had a benefit unknown to pioneers. It is a good source of vitamins A and C, as well as minerals.

For greens, Mrs. Crowder used dandelions, lamb's quarters, and redroot. Lamb's quarters is a weed that can grow up to two feet in height. Its young shoots were gathered in the spring, and its growing tips could be used at any time. It is another good source of vitamins A and C, as well as proteins and minerals. The dandelion leaves would have better been eaten in a salad than as potherbs, as the raw leaves are a good source of vitamin A. The redroot was probably pigweed, a plant that can grow up to six feet tall. Its leaves were generally used as greens when the plant was growing in the spring. Pigweed seeds could be ground and used in pancakes. Hunting provided a good supply of meat. Wild fowl were plentiful in the region, and in the first winter the Crowders ate many ducks, wild geese, cranes, and prairie chickens.[45]

By the 1860s, although there were still many newcomers in Iowa, rural abundance was becoming more common than scarcity. Emily Hawley Gillespie, who was born in Michigan in 1838 and lived in rural Iowa as a married woman in the early 1860s, gives a good idea in her journal of why many pioneers shunned the hardship of the long trek to new lands in the Far West. In Iowa it was now possible to have meat throughout the year without depending on the salt pork laid down at the beginning of winter, and Mrs. Gillespie's daily cooking reflected this. Among the meals she served were meat stew with dumplings, an old rooster (killed by her husband for them to have on their wedding anniversary), chicken pies, and spareribs.

Mrs. Gillespie did not even mention cooking what had been the everpresent salt pork, perhaps because she did not think it worth mentioning. They certainly still had it, as she accidentally fed salt meat to her turkeys and killed eighteen of them. Also, the crullers she made in January 1863 were undoubtedly fried in the lard from a recently slaughtered pig. By this time the wild turkeys had gone, and if they wanted turkeys, settlers raised their own. There were ample vegetables, and in the fall of 1866 the Gillespies' cellar was well stocked with fifteen bushels of potatoes, a barrel of

45. E. May Lacey Crowder, "Memoirs," in Riley, ed., *Prairie Voices*, 169–83.

onions, carrots, beets, and pumpkins. In making her own preserves, Mrs. Gillespie made use of the peaches that had been ever-present since the first settlers had moved into the Mississippi valley. She made both preserved and pickled peaches, as well as melon preserves. Like most farm wives, Mrs. Gillespie also made her own butter and cheese and raised a little money from them. In August 1866 she went into town and sold over twenty-five pounds of butter. She was able to make pies and tarts rarely seen by early pioneers, and celebrated a wedding anniversary with "a nice . . . cake." Perhaps the only reflection of an earlier, more stringent time comes in her journal when she mentions that when a man shot a blackbird, she cooked and ate it and thought it was good. Blackbirds were not typical even for frontier diets.[46]

Carving out new farms continued in the eastern woodlands and prairies through most of the nineteenth century. In the years after the Civil War, settlers were still taking up land claims in Ohio. Often the land was less desirable than earlier, but many were willing to accept this in order to avoid settling in an unfamiliar environment far to the west. There was a constant overlap in the movement of settlers across the American continent. The coming of statehood was often just the beginning of the main settlement and transformation of the land in any region. Those who came later to any area were much less likely to suffer the pangs of hunger that often beset the first settlers, but if they had few resources they still faced an arduous task of making a success of their farms and feeding their families. For those who hoped to find a richer and more abundant land, or who were simply restless, long horizons beckoned. Before most of the eastern woodlands and prairies had been conquered, many had pressed on across the continent.

46. Emily Hawley Gillespie, in Cathy Luchetti, *Home on the Range: A Culinary History of the American West* (New York: Villard Books, 1993), 141–44.

# *Part 2*

## Explorers and Trappers

# CHAPTER 3

# Game on Every Side

> The dog now constitutes a considerable part of our subsistence and with most of the party has become a favorite food.
>
> Meriwether Lewis, in the Rockies, 1806

T he patterns of eating formed over the long process of settling the eastern woodlands changed when American explorers, traders, and settlers advanced into the plains and mountains of the trans-Mississippi West. For the most part, the Great Plains had insufficient rainfall for the type of agriculture the settlers had long practiced. Mineral resources in the Rocky Mountain system would eventually make some pioneers wealthy, but many farmers were not so fortunate. Much of the mountain land was unsuitable for farming, and the flat expanse of the Great Basin needed irrigation before it could be made productive. California was more promising, but, in the south, lack of rain presented great problems for farmers. Only the Oregon country in the far Northwest offered the prospect of farming and eating in a manner that had become customary in the eastern woodlands.

American penetration and knowledge of the Far West began in dramatic fashion at the time when the United States was acquiring a vast area of the trans-Mississippi West in the Louisiana Purchase from Spain. In June 1803, President Thomas Jefferson instructed Meriwether Lewis to explore the Missouri River and its tributaries with the object of finding the most direct water link across the continent to the Pacific Ocean. Lewis and his partner, William Clark, between May 1804 and September 1806 commanded a small party of fewer than fifty men on an epic trek from St. Louis to the Pacific and back. The main group of soldiers was accompanied by hunters and by an Indian woman, Sacajawea, who joined the party on the Missouri. This was the first and most spectacular of a series of government-sponsored expeditions into the Far West that continued through much of the nineteenth century.[1]

The explorers expected to get much of their food by hunting and also took a supply of fishhooks and line, but Lewis stocked up on provisions before setting out. These included eleven bags and four barrels of hulled corn, thirty half-barrels of flour, seven bags and four barrels of biscuits, seven barrels of salt, fifty kegs of salt pork, a bag of peas, a bag of beans, two bags of sugar, one of coffee, six hundred pounds of "Grees," a keg of lard, and over one hundred gallons of whiskey. A more unusual item was nearly two hundred pounds of portable soup. Portable soup had been in use since the first decades of the eighteenth century. It was made by boiling a large quantity of meat for a considerable time to reduce the liquid to a syrup or paste and then drying the paste until it was hard. The cook could later rehydrate it with boiling water. Various flavorings could be added in the process of boiling. The portable soup for the Lewis and Clark Expedition was prepared in Philadelphia and packed in canisters.[2]

In mid-May 1804, the expedition set off up the Missouri from its camp north of St. Louis. The first stage of the journey, which took until late October, was to the Mandan Indian villages in what is now North Dakota. Soon after setting out, Lewis issued orders to regulate the issuing and cooking of provisions. The men were formed into five separate messes, and daily provisions were issued each evening after making camp. Some of the food cooked at that time by the different messes was saved for the following day, as no cooking would be allowed while the men were on the march. Provisions were to be varied over a three-day cycle—on the first day hominy and "grece," on the second day pork and flour, and on the third day cornmeal and pork. No pork was to be issued when fresh meat was available. "Grece" was a basic part of the diet, and on June 12, when the men met a hunting party, they bought three hundred more pounds.[3]

In these first months of the expedition, the men had a great quantity of fresh meat. It was usually venison, but the venison was quite often supplemented with bear meat. Through June the yield of deer was high—the

1. Jefferson to Lewis, June 20, 1803, in Donald Jackson, ed., *Letters of the Lewis and Clark Expedition, with Related Documents, 1783–1854* (Urbana: Univesity of Illinois Press, 1962), 61–66.

2. Moulton, ed., *Journals of the Lewis and Clark Expedition*, 2:217–18; Jackson, ed., *Letters*, 69–97; Stephen Ambrose, *Undaunted Courage: Meriwether Lewis, Thomas Jefferson, and the Opening of the American West* (New York: Simon & Schuster, 1996), 125–26, 133–34; Eldon G. Chuinard, *Only One Man Died: The Medical Aspects of the Lewis and Clark Expedition* (Glendale, Calif.: A. H. Clark Co., 1979), 160; Alan Davidson, *The Oxford Compansion to Food* (Oxford: Oxford University Press, 1999), 625.

3. Moulton, ed., *Journals*, 2:254–58, 294.

hunters killed seven on the fourth, seven on the eighth, and two on the eleventh (as well as two bears). This pattern continued in the following weeks. On the twenty-fourth, there were "imence" herds of deer on the surrounding prairies. The meat that could not be eaten immediately was cut into strips, impaled on sticks close to the fire, and dried for jerky. Fresh meat, hominy, and lard made up a great part of their diet, with some jerked meat and salt pork when fresh meat was occasionally unavailable.[4]

Most of the water they drank was taken from the Missouri River. Clark blamed this muddy water for the boils and diarrhea that were prevalent in the party, but it seems likely that gorging on great quantities of fresh meat may also have been part of the problem. They had no milk, so the men's only alternative to river water was the daily gill of whiskey each of them received. A gill was four or five ounces, hardly enough to satisfy the men's taste for liquor. Late in June, the soldier guarding the whiskey barrels succumbed to temptation and got drunk with a friend. The two were immediately court-martialed and given one hundred lashes and fifty lashes each.[5]

By July, Lewis was becoming concerned at the way in which the men were wasting provisions. The seemingly never-ending stream of fresh meat had given the men the idea that no caution was necessary. Lewis feared what might lie ahead. On July 8, orders were issued naming one man in each of the messes to be responsible for "judicious consumption" of provisions and for cooking them in "such manner as is most wholesome and best calculated to afford the greatest proportion of nutriment." The man in charge was also to decide what proportion of the provisions should be eaten at the three meals in the day.[6]

In midsummer, as the expedition continued upstream, wild fruit was readily available for those who wanted it. Clark's birthday at the beginning of August was celebrated with a special meal of a saddle of fat venison, elk, and a beaver tail, followed by cherries, plumbs, raspberries, currants, and grapes. To some extent, wild fruits took the place of vegetables. In mid-July, the men stored cherries in a whiskey barrel, and in the following month fruit was gathered regularly. Some of it was new to them. On August 21, Clark found "a verry excellent froot" resembling the red currant, and a few days later he gathered various fruits, including grapes, blue currants, and

4. Ibid., 2:276, 277, 286, 293, 294, 320.
5. Ibid., 2:329–30, 352, 378; Ambrose, *Undaunted Courage*, 147–48; Chuinard, *Only One Died*, 221–22.
6. Moulton, ed., *Journals*, 2:359–60.

plums. The plums came in three varieties—two yellow and one red. Clark particularly liked the flavor of the yellow.[7]

Elk, beaver, wild turkey, and geese now provided a change from venison, and the expedition was about to reach the buffalo country. By late August, numerous herds of buffalo were visible from the boats, and in September antelope began to appear in considerable numbers. Although always called antelope, they were actually pronghorns, the fastest game in North America.

Fish also provided an important element in the diet. Fat catfish were plentiful, and Clark said they could be caught at any time. From the surplus fat of one, they obtained a quart of oil. In the middle of August they made "a Drag" out of willows and bark and caught over three hundred fish of different varieties—pike, bass, salmon, perch, red horse, and catfish. On the next day, Lewis took twelve men to a pond and creek and caught about eight hundred fine fish. Over half of them were catfish, but there were also numerous buffalo fish and pike as well as a scattering of other types. At the end of August, Sgt. John Ordway wrote, "The Missouri river affords us pleanty of fish, & the Country pleanty of all kinds of Game."[8]

In mid-September, two of the men followed a tributary of the Missouri for twelve miles and reported that they saw great herds of buffalo, deer, elk, and antelope in every direction. As there was so much game, and because some of the buffalo they killed were of very poor quality, they often took only a few selected parts, most often the tongues and the marrow bones. Even in the midst of all this food, it was possible to go hungry. George Shannon became separated from the party and did not manage to rejoin it for over two weeks. He had a gun but no bullets. He managed to kill one rabbit by using a piece of hard stick in place of a ball but otherwise survived by eating grapes.[9]

While game was abundant, Lewis and Clark continued to take the precaution of having meat preserved. On September 8 the men jerked the meat from two buffalo, two elks, four deer, three turkeys, and a squirrel; and on the eighteenth all the venison from a kill of ten deer. The jerky was a precaution for the future, but it was also immediately useful for the hunters. They took jerky and biscuits with them on the hunt. Lewis and two hunters washed down one snack with rainwater from a small pool.[10]

7. Ibid., 2:380–81, 433, 498, 505; 3:14; 11:41; Ambrose, *Undaunted Courage*, 152; Chuinard, *Only One Man*, 225–26.

8. Moulton, ed., *Journals*, 2:426–27, 483, 485–86; 3:7, 11, 44, 70–73; 9:46.

9. Ibid., 3:66, 77; 9:58.

10. Ibid., 3:55, 81, 87.

In August, the party began to meet Indians, and these encounters became more numerous as the expedition advanced farther up the Missouri. The meetings were friendly, and there was an exchange of gifts, with Lewis and Clark regularly sending a few presents to make it clear that no hostility was intended. A party of Otoes and Missouris was given roasted game, pork, flour, and meal, and parties of Sioux received provisions, tobacco, and some cooking kettles. In return the Indians gave watermelons and meat. The explorers were also treated to dog meat, which was looked upon as a delicacy by some tribes. By the end of the expedition, dog meat was enjoyed by most of the American party.[11]

The men of the expedition soon were given ample evidence that the diet of these Indian tribes went far beyond meat. In mid-October, the Arikaris supplied the explorers with bread made of corn and beans, boiled corn and beans, squash (the Arikaris had three types under cultivation), and dried pumpkins. The Arikaris had cultivated enough corn to present the expedition with ten bushels.[12] Throughout the journey, the supplies that the explorers had brought with them, and the yield from hunting, were added to or replaced by food obtained from the Indians. At times it was their only salvation.

The explorers spent the whole winter of 1804–1805 at the Mandan villages, encamped in huts they built within what became known as Fort Mandan. Soon after they arrived, the Indians brought corn and dried pumpkins as gifts. The Mandans, like the Arikaris, had a varied diet. It included game along with corn, beans, and squash, which they regularly cultivated, and a variety of wild roots and berries, which they collected.

In the months before they could move on, Lewis and Clark hoped to preserve the provisions they had brought with them by obtaining foodstuffs from the Mandans and by hunting. At first the yield from hunting was good. On November nineteenth the hunters brought in thirty-two deer, twelve elks, and a buffalo. The men had built a smokehouse, and meat that was not immediately needed was hung there. Through December, the most common meat was buffalo, but they also ate antelope, elk, and venison. Later in the winter, they had to depend a great deal on venison and elk, as buffalo became very scarce. In continued fear of what might lay ahead, they made only sparing use of their salt pork.

At Christmas, the men had to be satisfied with a distribution of a little

11. Ibid., 3:16, 17, 21–24, 28–31, 111–13, 116; 11:87; Chuinard, *Only One Man,* 244–45; Ambrose, *Undaunted Courage,* 162.

12. Moulton, ed., *Journals,* 3:158–64; 9:79; Ambrose, *Undaunted Courage,* 178–80; Chuinard, *Only One Man,* 248–52.

flour, dried apples, pepper, an extra issue of brandy, and a few other items. At times, the weather became too bitter to hunt, and it was not always easy to find game. Early in January, three hunters, after killing nothing for two days, killed and ate a wolf. They "relished it pretty well, but found it rather tough." Early in February, a hunting party led by Clark brought in forty deer, sixteen elks, and three buffalo, and later in the month Lewis came in with two sleighs loaded with meat from a kill of thirty-six deer and fourteen elks. Some of the animals were so thin that they were largely unfit for use.[13]

By midwinter, Mandan supplies became essential, and in trade the explorers were able to provide services to the Indians, both by treating their sick and by doing blacksmith work. Late in December, when Lewis treated an abscess on an Indian child, the child's mother offered as much corn as she could carry in return for medicine. During the rest of the winter, Indians regularly visited the camp to trade food for services. By the end of the year they were coming every day, and the party's blacksmiths mended their hoes and axes in return for corn.

At times, the Mandans prepared some of their own dishes for the explorers. Just before Christmas, an Indian woman boiled a mixture of pumpkins, beans, corn, and chokecherries (with the stones in). Clark commented that this dish was considered a treat by the Mandans, and he thought it "paletable." The Indians also introduced the explorers to their bread, which they made of a mixture of parched corn and beans molded into round balls. The corn was picked in the summer when it was in the milk, boiled, and dried for winter use.[14]

On April 7, 1805, the explorers left their fort to proceed up the Missouri. They had survived the winter by hunting and by eating corn supplied by the Mandans. This had enabled them to save their own parched corn, dried portable soup, and much of their pork and flour. They now had with them the famous Sacajawea, an Indian woman of the Shoshone tribe, who was to be of great help when they reached her people in the Rockies. She also proved of immediate assistance in her knowledge of wilderness food. Two days after leaving Fort Mandan, when they stopped for dinner, Sacajawea went out to look for caches of wild Jerusalem artichoke roots. These tubular roots were gathered and stored in large quantities by mice, and the Indians used sticks to find them and dig them up. They provided a valuable vegetable addition to the constant meat. A few days later, the explorers

13. Moulton, ed., *Journals*, 3:199–202, 218, 225–26, 236, 238, 253, 292–95, 299; 10:69; 11:113; Chuinard, *Only One Man*, 256, 261.
14. Moulton, ed., *Journals*, 3:260, 261, 264, 298; 9:106–7; Chuinard, *Only One Man*, 261–62.

found a great quantity of small wild onions, some of which they cooked and enjoyed.[15]

Game was scarce in the first days after the expedition left the Mandans. Lewis blamed this temporary scarcity on the constant hunting in the area by the Indians. On April 11, the explorers had their first fresh meat in several days—a dinner of venison, beaver tail, and biscuits. They had hoped to save the biscuits for harder times but were forced to eat them because they had been soaked a few days before when a canoe filled with water.

These biscuits were usually called "ship's biscuits" or "hardtack." They were made of unleavened flour and cold water. The ingredients were kneaded, baked, and then slowly dried in an oven. Each biscuit was usually round and quite large, weighing half a pound or more. They would keep for a year or more if kept dry.[16]

Beaver, which could be as big as fifty or sixty pounds, became more numerous as they proceeded upriver, and their flesh, particularly the tails, was much favored by the men. Lewis agreed with them, and he also liked the liver. He thought boiled beaver tail resembled the best parts of codfish. Beaver tail was always one of their most popular meals. Clark wrote that the beavers he saw in this part of the Missouri were more abundant, larger, and fatter than he had seen anywhere.[17]

As they traveled up the Missouri toward the Yellowstone, there were "immence quantities" of game in every direction, and over the following weeks it could be slaughtered at will. It was "very abundant and gentle." At the end of a long winter, much of the meat was of inferior quality, but, unpalatable or not, great quantities were eaten. The men's appetites offset the problem of quality, and they could be highly selective. Buffalo calves, which were now becoming available, provided a special treat. Lewis, who generally showed a greater interest in food than did Clark, thought buffalo calf meat was delicious, "equal to any veal I ever tasted."[18]

In late April, they reached the Yellowstone and found game everywhere: buffalo, elks, deer, antelope, and beaver, as well as geese, ducks, and a few swans. On May fourth, Lewis passed great herds without shooting as they had "an abundance of meat on hand." The explorers preferred choice parts of adult buffalo, buffalo calves, venison, and beaver tails. Elk and antelope

15. Moulton, ed., *Journals*, 4:7–16, 25–26.

16. Ibid., 4:21–22; Frank A. Kennedy, "The Biscuit Industry," in *1795–1895: One Hundred Years of American Commerce*, ed. Chauncey M. DePew (New York, 1895), 448.

17. Moulton, ed., *Journals*, 4:25, 27, 32, 48, 54, 62; Chuinard, *Only One Man*, 277–78.

18. Moulton, ed., *Journals*, 4:36, 48, 55, 57, 78; 11:139.

meat were less favored. The explorers were seeing their first grizzlies and were awed by their size. One they killed was skinned and divided, its fat boiled and the oil put in kegs for future use. A large bear provided several gallons of oil. For some time fish had been scarce, but by June it was again becoming generally available.[19]

Ordway commented early that month that there was so much meat that "we do not trouble ourselves to catch fish," but that was not true for all the party. Ordway also mentioned that another man had caught "a considerable quantity of fish," mostly catfish. Trout were available, as well. In the middle of June, under the direction of Lewis, the men caught and dried numerous trout.[20]

As wild berries and fruits were not yet ripe, the men lived mainly on meat, still trying to preserve flour and corn for possible future difficulties. Variety continued to be provided by Sacajawea and by the Indians they encountered. Sacajawea dug up a good amount of an edible root called white apple (or breadroot). It was abundant in the area and was used in a variety of ways by the Indians. They boiled it with meat, and also, after boiling it, they mashed it and mixed it with buffalo grease and berries to form a pudding. For winter use, they dried it and pounded it into a powder, which was added to soups.

The explorers were also able to vary their diet with dried wild cherries. The Indians of this region made extensive use of purple-red chokecherries, the most abundant of all American wild cherries. They ate them in a variety of ways—freshly picked, boiled with roots or meat, or dried and pressed into small cakes for winter use. Fresh chokecherries were not yet available, as they did not ripen until July, but the explorers were able to obtain dried cherries from the Indians. Even with these additions to their diet, the men of the expedition continued to suffer from boils, skin eruptions, and stomach upsets.[21]

Meat was what the men of the expedition wanted, and in May the French-Canadian Touissant Charbonneau gave them a delicacy much-loved by the fur traders—*boudin blanc*. This was a type of sausage made from buffalo meat. About six feet of the lower part of the gut of the buffalo was roughly cleaned out to serve as the casing, and a filling was made of finely chopped buffalo meat from under the shoulder blades mixed with suet from the buffalo kidneys, flour, salt, and pepper. The sausage was first

19. Ibid., 4:66–75, 88, 90, 108, 113, 141, 286–87; 9:163.
20. Ibid., 9:163; 11:199.
21. Ibid., 4:125–26, 129, 145–46; Chuinard, *Only One Man*, 221–22; Ambrose, *Undaunted Courage*, 222–23.

boiled, then fried in bear's oil until brown. Lewis referred to this as one of the great delicacies of the wilderness.[22]

In May, the explorers saw and killed their first bighorns, the wild sheep that roamed mountain slopes. Clark thought their meat was inferior to venison but better than antelope. Any meat was better than none. Lacking buffalo, venison, elk, or beaver, the men ate what they could kill. On June 5, "to make shure of our suppers," they killed what they called burrowing squirrels. These were either ground squirrels or gophers. The men thought the meat was "well flavored and tender."[23]

At this stage of their journey, the explorers could usually still afford to be choosy. Often when they killed an elk, they took only the marrow bones. On June 11, they had a "feast" of them. Lewis could not eat because of a violent stomach pain, but he was well enough two days later to eat a "really sumptuous" meal of humps and tongues of buffalo, marrowbones, fine trout, parched meal, pepper and salt.[24]

They still feared—correctly—that this happy state of affairs could not last, and that there might be problems on their return journey. To prepare for the future, and to lighten their load, they took the precaution of leaving a cache with various supplies, including kegs of flour, pork, and parched corn. In mid-June, as they approached the Great Falls of the Missouri, hunters were sent out to kill as many buffalo as they could from the great herds that were all around them. They also killed deer. Lewis wanted to lay in a large quantity of dried meat to feed the men while they toiled in the arduous task of portaging around the falls.[25]

On the evening of the twenty-fifth, two hunters alone brought in eight hundred pounds of dried meat with one hundred pounds of tallow, and on the following day Lewis cooked for the men. He boiled a large quantity of the dried buffalo meat and made each man a large suet dumpling "by way of a treat." On July 4, the men were treated to the last of the whiskey they had brought with them, and the explorers sat down to a dinner of bacon, beans, suet dumplings, and buffalo.[26]

Indians had told the explorers that soon after passing the falls they would leave the buffalo country and that game would become much scarcer when they reached the Rockies. Lewis was concerned because they had often been using four deer, an elk, and a buffalo in twenty-four hours. In

22. Moulton, ed., *Journals,* 4:131.
23. Ibid., 4:193–98, 258–59.
24. Ibid., 4:277–78, 287.
25. Ibid., 4:269–72, 274–75, 283–89, 296–97, 317–18; 11:193.
26. Ibid., 4:331, 333–34, 362; Chuinard, *Only One Man,* 296; Ambrose, *Undaunted Courage,* 247.

the hope of making up for any future lack of game, the hunters, in addition to ordinary jerky, made pemmican. This was a food much favored by the Indians, especially when they traveled. Pemmican was made by drying buffalo or other meat and pounding it into a powder, which was then mixed with berries and melted fat. The party was still trying to reserve its flour, parched meal, and corn.[27]

By the middle of July, the arduous portage was over, and the explorers continued west, carrying with them a large stock of fat and dried meat and fish. The day after the expedition left the portage, Jefferson's Virginia must have seemed an eternity away to Lewis as he sat by a camp fire and for the first time ate a buffalo's small intestines. He had them Indian-style, cooked over the fire without cleaning, and he liked them. At home in Virginia, Lewis's mother used to make hams so tasty that Jefferson's overseer at Monticello used to get a few from her for Jefferson's "special use." In the following month, Virginia must have seemed even more of a dream, for Lewis saw hungry Indians fall upon a deer they had killed and eat its kidneys, melt (spleen), liver, paunch, and intestines raw. A great advantage of this—unknown at the time—is that the innards, particularly raw, provide a full range of vitamins, even vitamin C.[28]

For those men who were willing to vary the meat diet, there were now ample berries and fruits nearing ripeness. By mid-July, there was a "great abundance" of yellow, purple, and black currants, as well as serviceberries, ready for eating. There were also chokecherries and two species of gooseberries, but these were still not yet ripe. Lewis particularly liked the yellow currants, which he thought better than those in gardens in the East, and he soon found a black currant that he liked even better than the yellow. Clark also relished the various currants and berries. In July and August the explorers had all the berries they wanted to eat. They also found "great quantities of white crisp and well flavored" wild onions.

Sunflowers were now in bloom all around them. The Indians of the Missouri, particularly those who did not cultivate corn, used the seeds to make a kind of bread and to thicken their soup. For the bread they dried the seed, pounded it into a meal, and added enough marrow fat to make it into a dough. Lewis found this palatable. At times the Indians added a little water to the powdered meal and drank it.[29]

Variations to the regular diet were particularly welcome because game

27. Moulton, ed., *Journals*, 4:354, 377, 379; 5:103.

28. Ibid., 4:382–86; Marshall Fishwick, "Thomas Jefferson," in *The American Heritage Cookbook* (New York: American Heritage Publishing Co., 1964), 140.

29. Moulton, ed., *Journals*, 4:385, 391–92, 414, 417; 10:121, 126; 11:294–95.

was becoming scarcer. On July 31, when nothing was killed, one of the men commented in his journal that they were out of fresh meat, "which is very uncommon to us, for we have generally had double as much as we could eat." After two days in which their only kill was one beaver, they killed and ate two elk, a meat they probably would have avoided a month before.[30]

On August 12 the explorers reached the Continental Divide. They were no longer seeing buffalo. Their usual kills were deer or antelope, and after the riches of just a few weeks before, the men were disappointed in the quality. Antelope was never a favorite with them, and fish was about to take the place of the constant meat. For a time they went hungry. On August 13 an Indian gave Lewis a piece of roasted salmon (the first he had seen), but for the next two days he had only a little paste of flour and berries, some dried berry cakes given by the Indians, a kind of flour and berry pudding, and flour stirred into a little boiling water.[31]

In the next three months, the party made its way from the Continental Divide to the sea. Gorging on fresh meat, which had been the pattern at meals in the summer of 1805, came to an end. Though they still ate some meat, fish became an essential part of their diet, and the support and friendships of the Indian tribes they encountered became essential. The new pattern became apparent on August 19 and 20. Except for one beaver, their fresh food was trout, caught with "a sein" made of willow brush. Shoshone Indians gave the visitors salmon and chokecherries, and, in return, Clark gave them a little salt pork. The Indian gifts almost certainly signified hospitality rather than abundance, as Lewis on the following day wrote that a group of Indians they met were half-starved. Although the explorers had no fresh meat, they gave the Indians a good meal of boiled corn and beans and most of over five hundred trout that they had caught with a net made of bush. Lewis also gave the chief a few dried squashes that he had bought from the Mandans.[32]

In the following weeks, they ate anything that was available—a few geese, a beaver, "phesents," grouse, a little parched corn, berries, and mostly salmon. Pheasants are not native to North America and only became prevalent in the United States later in the nineteenth century. Possibly these "phesents" were white-tailed ptarmigan, native to the high Rockies. It was a great treat when they shot a few deer. Clark commented that he had eaten no meat for eight days. On September 3, John Ordway wrote in

30. Ibid., 5:20, 26; 9:199–200.
31. Ibid., 5:74, 83, 87, 95, 97; Chuinard, *Only One Man*, 307.
32. Moulton, ed., *Journals*, 5:119, 126, 130, 138, 144.

his journal that they ate the last of their pork and "lay down wet hungry and cold."[33]

In these weeks in September, the abundance they had enjoyed earlier in the expedition changed to near starvation. On September 14, with their hunters again unsuccessful, the men rehydrated a little of the soup they had brought with them and killed one of their colts. Ordway said that it ate "verry well." On the following days, with the hunters bringing in only pheasants, they killed two more colts and drank a little more of the portable soup. As there was no water, they melted snow to mix with it. On the twentieth, Ordway wrote that they were "half Starved and very weak."[34]

The situation was serious, and Clark and hunters went ahead, out of the mountains, to look for game in level country. That morning the main party finished the rest of a colt, and for dinner there was only condensed soup. They had little left except for a few canisters of soup and a small quantity of bear's oil. The next day they ate only the soup. Several men were suffering from dysentery, and many had boils and other skin eruptions. Before setting out on the frosty morning of September 20, they ate a few handfuls of peas, and "a little bears oil." They were saved by Clark and the hunters who killed a wild horse, ate some of it for breakfast, and left the rest for the main group.[35]

On September 21 the main party, led by Lewis, ate the remainder of the horse flesh, a few birds, a prairie wolf, and some crawfish. In the meantime, Clark's advance party reached a village of the Nez Percé Indians. They gave Clark a little of what they had—a small piece of buffalo meat, dried salmon, dried berries, and bread made out of roots—and on the following day when the hunters were unsuccessful Clark traded a few things he had in his pockets for dried salmon, bread, roots, and berries. These provisions were sent back to the main party, who ate the dried fish and roots with a crow they had killed.[36]

Until the explorers reached the rapids of the Columbia in late October, finding enough food continued to be a problem. Mainly, they ate dried fish and roots obtained from the Indians. They bought or caught a little fresh salmon but had very little large game. A deer that they killed on September 27 was divided between the sick and the Indians. On October 2, with no provisions, nothing to eat but roots and a small prairie wolf, and many

33. Ibid., 5:148–98; 9:217.
34. Ibid., 5:205, 207, 210–11; 9:223, 227.
35. Ibid., 5:211–13, 215–16; 9:227.
36. Ibid., 5:222, 226, 227, 228–29.

men sick, they were obliged to kill another of their horses. They were weak from lack of food, and Indian cooperation had become essential. To vary their diet, they now began to buy Indian dogs. Clark commented, "All the Party have greatly the advantage of me, in as much as they all relish the flesh of the dogs." Day after day they bought what they could from the Indians—dried fish, roots, berries, acorns, and an increasing number of dogs. Fresh fish were now rare, as salmon were out of season.[37]

In the last weeks of October, as they went out of the Snake River into the Columbia, there were signs of improvement. They shot a few ducks, and one of the party made what was described as "Some excellent beer" out of the remains of the root bread that had survived in their stores. As they descended the Columbia, they began to kill deer, but they were still eating dogs and squirrels. One of the men speared a salmon, and it was fried in a little bear oil given by an Indian chief. Clark pronounced it "one of the most delicious fish I have ever tasted." In November, as they traveled to the sea, they saw "great numbers of waterfowl" and regularly began to kill ducks, swans, and geese. Even now, some of the men were still buying dogs from the Indians. Earlier, in October, Patrick Gass had commented that "most of our people having been accustomed to meat, do not relish the fish, but prefer dog meat; which, when well cooked, tastes very well."[38]

On the shores of the Pacific, rain fell almost constantly while Lewis and Clark examined the area to decide where to spend the winter. While they looked, the men still depended heavily on dried fish, but they also had venison, a variety of waterfowl, and a few dogs and roots bought from the Indians. They also began to kill elk. They were still suffering from various stomach disorders.

The Indians continued to be friendly and helpful, and partly on Indian advice, the expedition decided to settle for the winter on the south bank of the Columbia, where there appeared to be ample game. In early December, they built crude Fort Clatsop, and they killed their first elk west of the Rockies. At one time they had spurned elk in favor of buffalo and beaver, but now it was welcome. In the weeks before Christmas they at last had enough elk and deer for the whole party to return to the largely meat diet the men preferred.[39]

Unlike the previous winter in the cold of Fort Mandan, the weather was quite mild, and there was constant rain. Some of the first elk they killed spoiled, and they built a hut to use as a smokehouse. Even after smoking,

37. Ibid., 5:231–96; 10:152–53.
38. Ibid., 5:315, 343; 6:9, 22, 31; 10:153.
39. Ibid., 6:93, 96, 105–9, 114–20.

the meat continued to deteriorate. Christmas dinner consisted of "pore Elk, So much Spoiled we eate it thro' mear necessity, Some Spoiled pounded fish," and a few roots. There was no alcohol left to use for toasts. On the twenty-ninth, Clark commented that the elk had become very disagreeable both to taste and to smell. A guard was ordered to keep fires alight in the smokehouse all the time they had meat there. Even with smoke under it around the clock, there was still difficulty keeping the meat fit for eating, and they now particularly enjoyed any meat from a fresh kill. On December 30, they had "a Sumptious Supper of Elks Tongues & marrow bones."[40]

Elk meat was usually very lean, and rich *fat* meat figured in their dreams. Lewis missed it much more than bread and had reached a point where he was not particular which meat it was. He said that dog meat, horse flesh, and wolf had, from habit, become equally familiar. The men found themselves reminiscing nostalgically about the days when they had been able to get plenty of dogs. Lewis said they had "now become extreemely fond of their flesh" and that when they had lived on dogs they had been healthier than at any time since leaving the buffalo country. He thought dog "an agreeable food" and said that he preferred it "vastly to lean Venison or Elk."

In the new year, the eagerness with which the men immediately ate any fresh meat made it necessary to change the method of distribution. Fresh meat had usually been divided among the messes, and it had been left up to them how much to eat fresh, and how much to cure. Often this had meant that it was rapidly used up when fresh. On January 12, when a hunter killed seven elk, it was decided that the meat would be dried before being doled out in small quantities.[41]

A major problem with returning to a largely meat diet was the lack of salt. This, like their other provisions, had been used up. A few weeks before Christmas, Clark went along the seacoast to find a suitable spot to set up a salt camp, and later in December men were sent there with five of the largest kettles to start making salt. This was a long and tedious process of boiling away seawater and gathering up the residue. They were able to make from three quarts to a gallon of salt a day. On January 5, they brought in about a gallon, and Lewis pronounced it "excellent, fine, strong, & white." The party had been out of salt since December 20. Lewis had very much missed it, but Clark announced that it was immaterial to him whether he had it or not.[42]

40. Ibid., 6:125–27, 135, 137, 138, 142, 145, 157; 10:184; 11:405, 406.
41. Ibid., 6:162, 166, 200.
42. Ibid., 6:116, 140, 166, 167; 9:262.